The Digitally Agile Researcher

Edited by

Natalia Kucirkova and Oliver Quinlan

Mc
Graw
Hill
Education

Open University Press

Open University Press
McGraw-Hill Education
8th Floor, 338 Euston Road
London
England
NW1 3BH

email: enquiries@openup.co.uk
world wide web: www.openup.co.uk

and Two Penn Plaza, New York, NY 10121-2289, USA

First published 2017

A catalogue record of this book is available from the British Library

ISBN-13: 978-0-335-26152-9
ISBN-10: 0-33-526152-3
eISBN-978-0-335-26153-6

Library of Congress Cataloging-in-Publication Data
CIP data applied for

Typeset by Transforma Pvt. Ltd., Chennai, India

Printed and bound by Bell & Bain Ltd, Glasgow

Fictitious names of companies, products, people, characters and/or data that may be used herein (in case studies or in examples) are not intended to represent any real individual, company, product or event.

Praise for this book

The Digitally Agile Researcher *is an important and welcome contribution to a growing literature on academic scholarship in the digital age. The book should be read by faculty and administrators alike, as it lays out a clear roadmap of the digital opportunities and challenges that researchers face and the support they require. If there is any hope for the future of the contemporary university, it will come through the communities we forge in new scholarly practices and the ways in which we negotiate digital society.* The Digitally Agile Researcher *will be instrumental in fostering those communities.*

Karen Gregory, University of Edinburgh, UK

Contents

List of editors and contributors

Helen Brown is Assistant Headteacher at Denbigh School and Director of the Denbigh Teaching School Alliance in Milton Keynes. In her role as Director, she facilitates the Outstanding Teacher Programme, supporting 'good' teachers in developing their practice to achieve 'outstanding' status. Previously, Helen was Head of the English and Media faculty for nine years, leading the faculty in significantly improving examination results at KS4 and 5. Recently, she has established and leads the Milton Keynes Secondary English network meetings to support department leaders across the local area. Helen provided Senior Leadership Team support for the development, enactment and evaluation of the 'Labcast' described in Chapter 9 of this edited collection.

Trevor Collins is a Research Fellow at The Open University's Knowledge Media Institute. Working in the area of Technology-Enhanced Learning, his research focuses on participatory approaches to technology innovation and organizational change within education. He is particularly interested in design-based research, which engages stakeholders as collaborators in an activity-centred design process. His publications are listed at: http://oro.open.ac.uk/view/person/tdc5.html.

Gareth Davies is a Research Associate at The Open University, UK. In his post he leads on the evaluation of a school–university partnership initiative project and a community engagement project. He is particularly interested in improving the quality of impact-evaluation for participatory design research projects carried out with a diverse range of communities. His publications are listed at: http://oro.open.ac.uk/view/person/gd3792.html.

Nicola Dowson is Library Senior Manager for research support at The Open University Library. Her role involves working in partnership across the university to develop products and services that support the university's research activity. She is particularly interested in developments in scholarly communication and their impact on how research is undertaken and communicated.

Carl Gombrich is Programme Director of UCL's Arts and Sciences BASc degree. He has degrees in Maths, Physics, and Philosophy and was a professional opera singer before joining UCL in 2002. Carl writes and speaks on themes related to interdisciplinarity and liberal arts and sciences. Recent engagements include keynotes at the Global Leaders in Arts and Sciences event at the Mori Arinori Centre in Tokyo and for the HEA in the UK. His interests include the future of work, notions of expertise, and the history of education. He is a member of the British Academy Working Group on Interdisciplinarity. He blogs at www.carlgombrich.org and is currently learning Mandarin in order to improve his understanding of education in China.

Jenny Hallam is a physics teacher working for Denbigh School in Milton Keynes. Jenny collaborated with Dr Simon Sheridan on the development, design and delivery of the scheme of work for the Labcast that is described in Chapter 9 of this edited collection.

Richard Holliman is Professor of Engaged Research at The Open University, UK. Through his teaching and engaged research, he explores relationships between academic researchers and non-academic stakeholders. He is particularly interested in the interplay between digital technologies and different forms of knowledge and expertise, and how the practices of engagement shape and frame contemporary research. His publications are listed at: http://oro.open. ac.uk/view/person/rmh47.html.

Natalia Kucirkova graduated in Psychology, holds a Masters in Research Methods and a Doctorate in Education. She worked at the Oxford University Education Department, pursued a pre-doctoral fellowship at the Harvard Graduate School of Education, and currently works as Senior Research Fellow at UCL, Institute of Education. Her research concerns innovative ways of supporting children's book reading, digital literacy, and exploring the role of personalization in early years. She has been commended for her engagement with teachers and parents at a national and international level.

W. Ian O'Byrne is an educator, researcher, and speaker. His research investigates the literacy practices of individuals as they read, write, and communicate in online spaces. Ian has been involved in a range of initiatives, including online and hybrid coursework, integrating technology in the classroom, ePortfolio systems, and supporting marginalized students in literacy practices. 'Ian actively creates and curates his digital identity through his main website, http://wiobyrne.com/.'

John J. Oliver is an Associate Professor of Media Management at Bournemouth University and an experienced academic who has published in international media and business journals. As an executive trainer, he has delivered programmes in Media Strategy to directors, managers, and producers from across the European audio-visual sectors. In the UK, he has delivered executive education to clients such as the BBC, ITV, Virgin Media, Sky, UKTV, Channel 4, FremantleMedia, and Bell Pottinger. A former Deputy President, and current Executive Board Member, of the European Media Management Association, he contributes to the management of the association's activities across 28 European countries.

Michael Parker is Membership Editor at The Conversation, a news analysis and opinion website written by academics working with journalists in order to bring academic expertise to the public.

Christian Payne Using mobile devices to document his surroundings, Christian specializes in creative technology and communications. Talking training and documenting, Christian also consults internationally and likes to travel light, sharing stories in real time. He overshares on @Documentally and writes a newsletter that can be found at http://Documentally.com/newsletter.

Victoria Pearson is a Senior Lecturer at The Open University, UK. Her research is in space and planetary science, specifically astrobiology and cosmochemistry, subjects at the interface between a variety of subject disciplines. She teaches on a range of interdisciplinary science and science and society courses and leads on equality and diversity initiatives across the institute's science curricula and environment. Her profile can be found here: http://www.open.ac.uk/people/vkp23.

Oliver Quinlan is Senior Research Manager for the educational charity the Raspberry Pi Foundation. He graduated in History, holds a Masters in Education, together with PGCE and PGCAP teaching qualifications. Starting his career as a schoolteacher, Oliver then became a Lecturer in Education at Plymouth University. In this role he was awarded the 'Vice Chancellor's Award for Inspirational Teaching'. Throughout his career Oliver has maintained what has grown into a well-known education blog, themes from which were developed into a book *The Thinking Teacher*, published in 2014. Both his blog and his online presences on networks such as Twitter have been integrated into his research practice and dissemination.

Mark Russell is Head of Faculty for Computing and Business and a computing teacher working at Denbigh School in Milton Keynes. From 2013–2015 Mark was a core member of the RCUK-funded Engaging Opportunities project. In his capacity as the Project Coordinator, Mark worked with local schools to increase the opportunities for students and teachers to work with researchers from The Open University and to engage them with aspects of contemporary research. Through this work Mark engaged with a wide range of researchers, collaboratively developing, enacting and evaluating school-university activities, including the Labcast described in Chapter 9 of this edited collection.

Simon Sheridan is a Project Officer working in the School of Physical Sciences at the Open University, UK. He is involved in the development and characterisation of instrumentation for the in-situ determination of the chemical composition of the atmosphere, surface and subsurface of major and minor solar system bodies. Simon collaborated with Jenny Hallam on the development, design and delivery of the scheme of work for the Labcast that is described in Chapter 9 of this edited collection. His profile can be found here: http://stem.open.ac.uk/people/ss27739.

Gemma Ware is Society Editor at The Conversation, a news analysis and opinion website written by academics working with journalists in order to bring academic expertise to the public.

Steve Wheeler is a learning innovations consultant at steve-wheeler.net and former associate professor at the Plymouth Institute of Education. He continues to research technology-supported learning and distance education, with a particular emphasis on the pedagogy underlying the use of social media and Web 2.0 technologies, and also has research interests in mobile learning and cybercultures. He is a prolific speaker and writer - his blog 'Learning with 'e's ' is a regular online commentary on the social and cultural impact of disruptive technologies, and the application of digital media in education, learning, and development.

Foreword

Agile thinking, like agile management, is quick, outward-looking, and adapts to changes in the wider world. The agile researchers in this book do this in a digital world, and more. They gather their ideas and their data in the open, develop their ideas in the open, and share their ideas openly, and they do it with the help of fast-evolving digital tools. Indeed, they adopted this way of working to develop the book, and an accompanying website. This is a far cry from the ivory tower of academia.

These authors are part of a worldwide movement that involves crossing boundaries to discuss research planned, in progress or completed with people who, coming from a different starting point, are likely to see it differently. This movement requires every participant to step outside their comfort zone to both listen and speak up in a less familiar territory. Courage and reflection are essential to benefit from drawing on knowledge held in different territories. The learning in this book comes from authors who've had that courage, and reflected on their journeys: the opera singer with degrees in Maths, Physics, and Philosophy; the BBC Science Media Fellow who became a professor; the academics who work across disciplines and with communities outside; and the journalists and academics who work together.

Reaching out in a digital era is both easier and more daunting, as communication through social media travels faster, travels further, and is irrevocable. The abundance of information, communications, and tools can be overwhelming, and guidance is available here. The authors offer help with frameworks, tools, best practice, and common pitfalls.

More importantly, in offering personal stories they model a way of advancing ideas incrementally by developing connections and provoking discussion long before those ideas warrant traditional academic publication. The like of departmental seminars and thought-provoking corridor conversations in the workplace are being enacted at a distance with blogs and Tweets to share ideas as they develop. Introductions are not with a handshake but a digital profile. Readers are encouraged to take charge of their own digital profile as they set out on their unique journey.

I share the authors' enthusiasm for crossing boundaries in the world of knowledge. As a teenager I wielded a trowel excavating a Roman villa, subsequently wore a white laboratory coat as an early career researcher, when a young mother, I advocated for childbearing women in health services research, and as an academic have involved people from outside of academia in shaping my social science studies. The importance and the challenge of crossing boundaries with research have spurred me to study the process formally. This is the book to help me enhance my work by developing my digital agility. I hope other readers are similarly encouraged.

Sandy Oliver
Professor of Public Policy
UCL Institute of Education
University College London

(Sandy is also Editor of *Research for All,* a peer-reviewed journal focusing on research that involves universities and communities, services or industries working together. *Free to readers, free to authors.*)

Preface

How did this book come about?

Oliver and I first met in 2014. I was working as Knowledge Transfer Partnership Associate at the literacy charity BookTrust and Oliver was a programme manager for Nesta's digital education projects. We were both committed to exploring ways in which digital technologies can transform education, but also the practices of researchers and educators. While the exact topics of the research projects we worked on were different (Oliver was managing a project on schools' use of digital technologies and I was researching children's digital books), there was a clear synergy in terms of how the research was communicated, shared, and conducted with the help of digital technologies and media.

The concept for this book was born out of our interest in the many new forms of digital scholarship and public engagement, and the challenges and opportunities they bring to researchers. During our work on the book, we discovered several new tools ourselves, and we have experimented with some of the ideas presented in the chapters. Oliver is a keen blogger and has been very active on Twitter and has set up his own newsletters. I have been inspired by one of the chapters to try out some video production and present my research in a more visual and accessible form. We hope that you might be inspired and adopt some selected practices as you read through this book.

It is worth pointing out that the practices and approaches described in this book carry various official names and even the contributors in this book use various terms and definitions to describe what we subsume under the umbrella term of 'digitally agile research'. You may come across terms such as digital engagement, engaged research, public engagement, impact, outreach or even 'real research', all which we consider to be connected to the shared goal of increasing the public awareness and practical usefulness of empirical research.

Why did this book come about?

To engage in research effectively means communicating findings to various groups. The era of presenting research findings to a small group of academic colleagues is over – all good funding bodies fund research that has a direct impact on society. The UK's National Coordinating Centre for Public Engagement (NCCPE) lists six key reasons for public engagement:

- to inspire school children, adults or families to take an interest in your subject area or discipline
- to disseminate the results of your research

- to involve the public in helping formulate a research question or project
- to consult the public on their views about your work
- to encourage people to help you do your research
- to collaborate with the public in developing and running a project or activity.

(Taken from: https://www.publicengagement.ac.uk/plan-it/why-engage)

There are several other organizations that help researchers with impact, dissemination, and public engagement, including Vertigo Ventures ('works with world-class academic institutions and professionals enabling them to plan, track and report impact') and Almetric ('tracks a range of sources to capture and collate this activity, helping you to monitor and report on the attention surrounding the work you care about').

Impactful and international public engagement would be hard to imagine without the help of digital technologies. Even if you organize a face-to-face event with a local school, you are likely to use several digital tools to arrange the visit and follow-up activities. For example, you could have a small blog site where you tell the students and their parents what your visit is about, or a Facebook forum for follow-up discussions with interested teachers, or you could create a small community around a Twitter hashtag related to your visit. Communication in the twenty-first century is often richer and more effective when it includes digital elements. In this hypothetical example, it would allow you to connect your visit to other researchers who might be visiting schools for a similar purpose across the world. It would allow you to create a community that can continue conversations beyond one short face-to-face visit. It would create a digital trace that can be included in the actual research analysis and strengthen your findings.

There is no doubt that digital technologies can be a double-edged sword in almost any context of use. When it comes to digital public engagement, there is a clear advantage of reaching out to international and wider research networks via the internet, and a clear disadvantage of spending precious research time on dissemination activities. However, the question is no longer whether to adopt digital media for public engagement but *how* to do so most effectively.

There are more and less effective ways of being a digitally agile scholar. Given that the technologies and software programs supporting digital engagement are new and being developed at a breakneck pace, often the only way to find out an effective way involves a trial-and-error approach. However, as a community, researchers can learn from each other and develop their own practices and culture around digital scholarship. In many respects, a community and culture of practice have been growing organically since the emergence of social media and blogging sites. Scholars and digitally agile researchers such as Jessie Daniels, for example, have been capturing these changes and documenting what it means to be a scholar in the digital age. This book adds to this trend by outlining clearly and openly some digital practices that can add both to the theoretical discussion and practical engagement in this area.

We do not pretend that participating in public engagement via digital media is pain-free and reducible to a set of practices. We asked our contributors to consider both the more and less effective ways of their chosen activity and to summarize the pros and cons in two sections ('best practice' and 'common pitfalls'), included at the end of the chapter. We focus on an arbitrarily selected set of practices that we found to be most popular, widespread, and that our contributors felt knowledgeable to write about.

Rather than presenting universal solutions, we wanted to offer some personal insights into how specific practices are executed and what motivates them. The choice of our contributors was guided by the belief that one of the best ways to learn is through examples and experiences of others. We chose authors who are themselves digitally active or agile and who were ready to share their personal journeys with others.

Who wrote this book?

Our contributors are former or current teachers, academics, scholars, journalists, and librarians. Their various backgrounds and eclectic approaches to public engagement reflect our shared view that there is no single, no specific profile of a digitally agile researcher. Digitally agile scholars can be at any stage of their career, and may be aiming for different goals. What unites them and hopefully brings you to this book is the interest in digital tools. Our contributors blog, tweet, and use Facebook multimedia to reach wider audiences. They marry scholarship with practice, to make an impact or ensure wider benefits of their research. They approach the theme of public engagement from various angles, with their own style and approach. We hope this diversity will highlight our intention to be inclusive and showcase the unconventional versatility and variety of digital engagement.

How did we write this book?

The individual book chapters do not offer a step-by-step guide for becoming a digitally agile researcher. This is because we don't think that one can become digitally agile by following a certain path. Rather, the journey will be individual for each reader and we encourage you to contextualize the ideas presented here within your own practice.

In many respects, the themes of agency, creativity, and resourcefulness run through all the chapters in this book and characterize the individual journeys of its contributors. Our contributors do not provide blueprints to follow but rather an honest account of the challenges they have encountered as well as the benefits they have accrued on the various journeys they have been on. They do provide practical tips and ideas for approaches, though, and the spirit of the book is for readers to identify the areas that are most interesting to them and have a go at developing them in their own practice. We hope the book is an enjoyable read in its entirety, but the real aim is for readers to take the advice and try it out. Digital agility will develop from practice, and getting started as soon as possible with some of the more practical advice will lead you to develop in this way. Our approach to writing the chapters was collaborative, we asked each other for feedback and shared thoughts via emails and blogs on the book's website http://www.digitallyagile.com/.

A word of caution . . .

Before we plunge on, we want to give a word of caution regarding the longevity of the advice and guidance represented in this book. Apps and sites appear and disappear and we cannot promise that the resources that we, or other contributors, mention in this book will survive in the long term. Similarly, with the best intentions in the world we could not have covered all the various tools and resources available to digitally savvy researchers today. What we have done instead is to point readers to some platforms and places where some of these resources can be found. We have endeavoured to portray practices that can survive the ebbs and flows of digital developments and that can be adapted to individual research fields and approaches. This book is therefore not a walk through various tools but rather the broader themes of how some digital tools can enrich scholarly practice, how they can help you conduct more engaging and impactful research, and disseminate it more widely.

As Carl Gombrich explains in Chapter 4, the examples of blogging and many other practices currently popular ought to be read as a snapshot, capturing the moment frozen in 2016/2017. To go beyond this moment means that you need to keep up-to-date by regularly browsing and discovering other platforms. This is unlikely to be a lonely endeavour though. Join the communities described and that you come across and you will find people identify new platforms and tools together, and any significant moves to different spaces are likely to be done by entire communities over time – after all, it is the communities of communication that bring values to most of the spaces described in this book.

We very much want to keep the collaborative spirit of this book and invite you to become part of this community: please let us know your thoughts by using the hashtag #digires on Twitter or Facebook or by contacting us by email and direct messages. Tell us what you like, which projects, approaches, and practices you are interested in and want to share with others. If the site we recommended no longer exists when you read this book, please accept our apologies and let us know. Equally, let us know when you find something exciting that you think other like-minded researchers might be interested in. The contributors and editors of this book are all on their own journeys into new ways of using digital tools just as you are.

We conclude by sharing some of our favourite projects and useful links.

Recommended resources

#A Minute CPD, Improve your digital skills one minute at a time. [https://1minutecpd.wordpress.com/]

Being a Scholar in the Digital Era: Transforming Scholarly Practice for the Public Good!, Jessie Daniels and Polly Thistlethwaite, published by Policy Press. [http://www.jessienyc.com/books.html]

Research for All journal, published by UCL IOE Press. [https://www.publicengagement.ac.uk/work-with-us/current-projects/research-all-journal]

The Guardian Follow the leaders, the best social media accounts for academics. [https://www.theguardian.com/higher-education-network/2016/mar/23/follow-the-leaders-the-best-social-media-accounts-for-academics?CMP=new_1194&CMP=]

Acknowledgements

The editors would like to thank all those who have contributed to the development of this book, including the individual chapter authors, online followers, and the book publisher.

Special thanks to Professor Richard Holliman for his incisive and valuable comments.

Changes to academic practice in the twenty-first century

Oliver Quinlan

Introduction

What does it mean to be a researcher in the twenty-first century? Some significant way into the era, we still find ourselves asking such questions. Researchers are not the only ones doing so; digital society is causing similar soul-searching across many professions and, indeed, many facets of life. The fast pace of technological and social change, our tendency to see new technologies as a mirror that cause us to look at ourselves in new ways, and the prescience of the date served to us by our calendar system lead to a strange combination of forward-looking enthusiasm and sometimes crippling 'future shock' (Toffler, 1973).

Here, I examine some of the key themes relevant to academic practice in the twenty-first century. There was an abundance of discourse around the turn of the century underpinned by a sense that western society was starting to change. At the time of writing in 2017, such discourse seems to be dispersing just, it seems, as we are really starting to get a feel for what the character of this century might be, in terms of both opportunities and challenges. The key theme, for academics and for us all, is change – change itself, change in the pace of change, change even in attitudes towards change, and how we respond to it. This change is most pressingly felt in some key areas. Changes in the abundance of information are key to researchers, given the knowledge focus of their work. Changes in communications have far-reaching effects, from how we communicate with each other to how our work reaches other groups in society. Changes in the tools that current technology brings allow new possibilities for productivity, but also challenges in terms of focus and compatibility with established practices. These more tangible themes of change result in more subtle changes in the relationships between subjects, conductors, and audiences of research, in the structures within which these groups participate, and in the social power and political forces that shape their experiences.

We celebrate the opportunities for communication that new technologies bring, but then often lament that the technology is used differently to how we foresaw. In academia, communications technologies were seen as having the potential for mobile, democratized learning, yet they are mostly used by the young to indulge the building of ever wider and more complex social circles rather than studying the traditional subjects we, older people, think are important. Such uses change at a blistering pace –even I, as a student of digital technologies in my early thirties, am left perplexed by the culture of Snapchat among contemporary teenagers.

The ephemeral promise of new technologies is easy to evangelize. After all, a future full of connections, opportunities, and possibilities is one that we can project any of our hopes and ideals onto. Conversely, it is also incredibly tempting to criticize, the emerging and experimental behaviours of people with these new tools are inherently varied in their effects. The pace of change is so fast that focusing our energies on the 'tried and tested' often seems very appealing.

This book is based on the perspective that there is a middle way for academics and researchers between evangelizing the new and sticking to tradition. Finding it requires cutting through both the technological utopianism and scepticism that often constitute the discourse around digital technologies. It is a challenging undertaking, but we believe that academics are well placed to take it on. Academics necessarily look towards the future of their field, developing new ideas and approaches, yet balance this with a strong criticality and respect for traditions hard won in the realm of experience and study. Despite some social and political movement towards a conception of universities as factories producing products of quantified research outputs and 'work-ready' young people, academia is still a place to explore what possible futures might look like and what they could mean to us. There are few areas that both welcome and require optimistic and critical experimentation as much as that of the agile use of digital technology.

Abundance of information

Access to 'the information superhighway' was one of the earliest visions of the internet as it began to become mainstream in the 1990s (Leadbeater, 2009). It is hard to argue that this hasn't been delivered, so much so that the term quickly moved from novel to unremarkable, to now seeming quaint. Yet it's easy to forget at this point the huge shift in access to information we have undergone, and the effect that this is having on academics.

If the essence of academic work is 'leaving no stone unturned', then the stones of literature have become infinitely easier to find since online databases sprung up to complement library stacks. Being just a keyword search away from a comprehensive set of papers and chapters that can be downloaded to read would have been unprecedented only a short time ago. The fact that this is also available in almost any location is an important change in allowing academic work to be easily accessible in different places and times. Searching for new material and reading can now take place around the other commitments of people's lives. However, the problem shifts from finding the stones to look under, to deciding which are most valuable to the skill of filtering has become hugely important in the environment of abundant information.

As the tools for getting hold of literature have become so much more comprehensive, so have those for keeping one's own collection of literature organized and easily accessible for synthesis and for writing. Reference and literature management tools now offer potential for tagging, searching, and often note-taking. Like any tools, they require some investment of time to develop familiarity and workflows, but with this commitment they offer huge benefits in terms of speed and access to literature over paper-based filing methods, which so often can devolve into the towering stack of papers covering a desk!

The time needed to access relevant materials and keep on top of the literature in a given area has been drastically reduced. Unfortunately, technological innovations have not yet managed to similarly reduce the time needed to actually read and understand this material.

As with many changes in technology, it could also be argued that technology has contributed to changing the culture. For those just starting out in their research careers, there can be little that is more intimidating than coming across a paper that begins with a strong assertion that contains as many words in brackets after it as are in the sentence itself, something that seems increasingly common in recent years. When literature is so widely accessible, the temptation, soon followed by the expectation, can become to never stop. The work that used to be put into searching the stacks becomes the work of reading every paper imaginable on a topic before feeling confident in one's coverage of it. Couple this with the fact that just reading one more paper can easily become an exercise in comfortable procrastination, and it can become a real challenge to move on from soaking in the warm bath of the literature to standing in the cold air and producing your own work.

For professional researchers in western institutions, the practical benefits of the abundance of information are huge, despite the challenges this can bring in terms of keeping up. For researchers in societies in other parts of the world, or not linked to large institutions, these changes are even more pronounced, as are the challenges bound within them.

For these groups of people, who lack the support of comparatively well-funded institutions, a comprehensive access to literature and information via institution libraries has until recently been relatively impossible. Now, digital information has the potential to radically reduce costs of access, making access possible for researchers in parts of the world where economic circumstances and infrastructure previously made it very difficult, and even to more casual researchers not linked to an institution but still keen to carry out enquiries of their own. In an increasingly complex world, some members of the public wish to expand their understanding of issues affecting their lives from robust and scientific sources, and sites such as The Conversation have been developed to support this, as is discussed by Gemma Ware and Michael Parker in Chapter 5. The key word here is 'potential', for there are still challenges to this democratization of access to knowledge. It is important to remember that computer and internet access are not universally inexpensive, and that in many parts of the world lack of infrastructure or cost of access can make even resources available 'free online' far from free to the end-user. Also, many academic resources are not provided free online. Although well-funded institutions often have widespread access to resources provided by academic publishers, the cost of this is often prohibitively high for those not a member of these few institutions. Indeed, as funding models shift, the cost of access to academic digital resources is becoming a point of debate even in countries with the most well-funded universities in the world (Van Noorden, 2013). Richard Holliman and colleagues explore this in more detail in Chapter 9.

Alongside these shifts is the movement for open academic publishing. Much academic work is funded by taxpayers across the world and there are those who argue that its outputs should be freely available. Some arguments for open publishing are based on such economics, while others explore the benefits in terms of moving forward a field when the largest number of researchers possible have access to its knowledge base. For these reasons and more, there are now many journals based on an open-access model. While these publications usually still adhere to a peer-review model for judging their content, they take advantage of the low costs of digital distribution to make access to their content free for researchers or indeed for anyone. Not all publishers are taking this route. With open access publishing still developing, in many fields the most established and highly rated journals are still those behind pay-walls.

The history of the internet has often been one of technological means moving more quickly than societal, or at least legal, precedents. Perhaps the most visible example of this has been the music industry, which has been hugely re-shaped by its response to the growth of illegal downloading of content. The traditional revenue model of physical album sales was challenged first by piracy of digital content, then by new models of legal online distribution. Whereas record sales used to fund promotional tours, now live shows often provide the funding for recording new content that engages fans and entices them to these events. The model has shifted hugely, and continues to do so with the challenges of new technologies, such as music streaming.

There are similar tensions now in the area of access to academic work. Sci-Hub is one example of a platform created to distribute pirate copies of academic papers to 'remove all barriers in the way of science' [https://scihub.org/], currently claiming a library of 58 million papers. They are in some senses to journals what 'Napster' was to music. The analogy only goes so far though. In this context, the justification is less about content being 'free as in beer' and more 'free as in freedom', with the potential benefits of free access framed around equity and innovation. Sci-Hub's website details the aims of fighting 'inequality of access' and both supporting the open access movement and opposing copyright and intellectual property laws for scientific and educational resources. Unlike open access journals, whose publishers aim to effect change through encouraging others to work with them to legally shift the model of access to knowledge, initiatives such as Sci-Hub do so by explicitly breaking the laws their founders disagree with (Bohannon, 2016). Such strong positions and willingness to take part in illegal actions illustrate just how much our global society is grappling with what the changes in access to information mean to us.

While engaging with such huge amounts of information can be a challenge for academics, it is even more so for those who cannot afford to dedicate the time and focus to the task that those involved in research can, or at least are expected to. Therefore, the role of the academic as a communicator of robust and reliable information has gained a new impetus. In a world of abundant information, we need curators more than ever. Helpfully for this role, we have also seen great changes in the tools and cultures of communication.

Abundance of communications

Changes to communication caused by the wide availability of digital tools and the internet are something that we still regularly reflect on across society. With so many types of digital communications and media, it is not just how we consume information that has changed, but how we interact with it, and with each other.

Perhaps most obvious is how we relate to each other in public, but communications have also had a huge impact on how academics relate to their peers. The focus required for conducting research can be isolating. In large universities even those sharing a building – or even an office – can be relatively unaware of the work that their colleagues are undertaking until it reaches publication. Conferences and other sharing events have long been used to expose our ideas to an audience of peers, whether inside our own institutions or further afield. These events are beneficial, but with the time and costs involved can be few and irregular. This very irregularity creates an occasion of such events, meaning much of the work being presented is polished, well prepared, and well on the way to completion, if not there already. Yet, what is often most useful in feedback from peers is that it is timely, delivered as you are mid-process, when adjustments can be made with the minimum of cost in terms of time and resources. Many academic institutions have facilitated this traditionally, with activities such as internal seminars, conferences, and research clinics. These can be very beneficial, although meeting face to face for an extended time with a large number of people on a regular basis is often a challenge.

Digital media afford both the speed to allow informal, ongoing sharing of process, and the wide reach to people who are well placed to give feedback. A quick question on a nascent idea on planning a study can be shared in moments on Twitter for feedback, and an emergent theme not yet fully clear can be described on a blog to invite identification of what has been missed. Such media can allow researchers to share their process as it is developing, and find a network of others who may be at a similar stage as themselves. Such connectivity allows sharing little and often, and asynchronous communications that can open up much more regular and ongoing communications with peers. The regularity can lower the stakes of such communications, allowing them to supplement more formal opportunities for gaining feedback on work in new ways. With some effort spent to build a network, and to share and offer one's own advice, the potential for useful and timely feedback from peers is vast. Ian O'Byrne and Steve Wheeler consider the activities needed to develop such methods in detail in Chapters 2 and 3 respectively, and with some investment of time all researchers should be able to benefit from a digitally enhanced version of the peer networks that academics have traditionally cultivated.

Many tools are available for digital networking, all with different affordances that shape the way they are used. Many academics are choosing to undertake peer-to-peer communication using public media such as Twitter. This brings both constraints and advantages. Clearly, public communications mid-research raise important issues of ethics regarding subjects, and challenges around how some view the sharing of findings before formal publication. There is a feeling in some quarters that sharing what you are working on too early could lead to others building on your work before it is ready, or even taking the idea of a study and using it themselves. However, sharing publicly can open up opportunities for serendipity that bring immense value. Many researchers sharing their developing ideas and research process online find that advice, conversations, and even opportunities open up as a result of this transparency. In Chapter 4, Carl Gombrich provides a specific example of how blogging about his developing thinking led to a career opportunity, and anecdotes such as this are shared frequently among the digitally active research community.

Such transparency also presents the second broad opportunity of online communication: opening up your research to the public. In building an online profile there is an obvious opportunity to share the published outputs of research with the public, linking to papers and presentations on a regular basis in blog posts or Twitter updates, and bringing the expertise and knowledge developed through research into online discussions. Many academics have built strong followings and online profiles as accessible and engaged experts in particular fields, brought into discussions by practitioners in their fields, journalists or even members of the general public. For example, Dr Tanya Byron is an active participant in online discourse on Twitter regarding the issues around young children growing up with digital technology. And Dr Ben Goldacre has become a regular contributor to print media and on television as a result of his work that includes blogging and producing a popular book, *Bad Science* (Goldacre, 2009).

There are other opportunities, however, arising from the ongoing sharing of research process and developing ideas. In this way, practitioners in your field or members of the public can gain insight into the research process. There is a concern that research outputs can be seen as impenetrable and beyond the grasp of those with a more casual interest. Sharing the process with which they are produced can make the area of academic work more understandable to others, providing a transparency and an engagement with the public that goes beyond just digital dissemination. This is new ground that is being explored by several authors in this volume and, when done well, it can help with linking researchers and the wider world, creating opportunities to deepen the perceived relevance and authenticity of your work.

There are some limitations to be noted here. Academic work necessitates complex and difficult cognitive work, and focus is key. It can be easy to be sucked in to the rolling nature of digital communications technology, and spend as much if not more time communicating than undertaking the focused work that leads to high-quality research. There are times in a project where timely feedback is important, and others when a deep focus is required. A genre of online commentary has grown around 'cults of distraction' created by our potentially always being in communication, and this is a particular danger to those whose work requires intense focus.

A key activity is to create a plan for how and why you want to make use of digital communications. Consider the stage of your career and how relatively useful it will be for you to connect with peers, influential academics and the general public. How you prioritize these audiences or contacts will shape your activity. For each audience, consider why you want to reach out to them and what benefits this will bring in the short, medium, and long term. Then consider how you might practically achieve these goals. This can be a complex area, and it is likely you will want to communicate with all these audiences in some way. It is worth creating a written plan or strategy for communications, and indeed your use of any broad set of digital tools. This may seem overly formal, but creating a written plan for yourself ensures you spend focused time thinking about it and the concrete act of writing down your goals can bring into relief ideas that can be unhelpfully vague when only considered in your head. Your goals and the activities you need to undertake to achieve them will change as your career develops, so return to this plan regularly and amend, reflect or start anew.

It need not be, though, with a reflective approach towards how you want to engage online, and the investment in this activity, you can reach a balance. The time you spend on communication tools can be focused on gaining the benefits described while not undermining the research process.

Abundance of tools

The very nature of tools has become complex with the advent of digital technologies. Some tools take the form of hardware devices that might fit the traditional definition of a tool. Others now exist solely in software that is used on multifunction devices. As software has become increasingly interlinked, sometimes a cluster of pieces of software can come together into a toolset or a workflow. Some of these software tools are designed for only a relatively small specific purpose, to be used alongside other tools. An example of this might be IFTTT.com, which exists solely to link together other services, passing blog posts to electronic reading apps or posting new articles to a Twitter feed automatically. Others are designed to be comprehensive environments for a particular type of work. For example, dedoose.com provides a number of tools for working with qualitative data from the coding and note-taking stages to thematic analysis. Scrivener provides a similarly comprehensive environment for writing, with different aspects of the tool designed for research and note-taking, planning and outlining, and writing and editing.

There is often a certain presumption of inevitability in discussions concerning digital technology, but simply picking up on the latest new tools will not in itself bring distinct benefits. In fact, in the worst cases they can encourage approaches that make work more challenging. What is needed is an intentional approach to workflows, a reflective look at tools and the roles they can play in the way you want to work.

The availability of digital tools is another of the big changes we face. Every week there are countless new apps, sites, and online tools, some free, some paid for. The specialist world of academia has less bespoke tools popping up than in the consumer world, but there is still considerable choice. Academics are also often encouraged to pick up general consumer technologies, particularly in the area of communications.

While tools may be free, there is always a cost, even if that is just the time and effort taken to learn how to use something and become effective in its use. This can be particularly true of consumer technologies that are being adapted for academic uses. One example of this is electronic reading devices. E-ink reading devices, such as a Kindle or Nook, are at first glance a technology that would seem to have many benefits for academics, with their overflowing bags of papers and books, and their need to regularly search for specific passages to cite in their work. However, search online for advice on using e-readers for academic reading and it soon becomes clear there is no clearly accepted or widely shared workflow. E-readers are designed for the more casual activity of reading for pleasure, their screens are too small to fit an entire document in the A4 pdf format of most journals, and highlighting and note-taking are possible but often cumbersome. There are some academics who swear by their e-ink readers, but to get to this position they have invested significant time developing their own workflows. Many of them use software such as library management tool Calibre to manage their collections of literature, and have found tools of techniques for converting their papers for the small screens.

Similar challenges exist for using tablet computers as tools for writing, and even on workflows for more specialist software such as reference managers, and data analysis tools. Sometimes this can be because specific tools are only of use for specific functions, or have particular ways of doing things that can be taken advantage of but also have to be worked around. In many cases, though, it comes down to a mixture of personal preference and the specific needs of certain types of work. This has always been the case, and researchers have always had different ways of approaching their workflows. The abundance of tools can seem overwhelming, but perhaps this is also partly because people are sharing and discussing them explicitly in greater numbers. There is something about digital tools and the modern culture of online communications that encourages many people to share how they do things. As someone new to a particular tool or area of work, some time spent reading up on this before investing the time yourself in developing a particular way of working can be beneficial. Do remember, though, that, as in the case of e-ink reading devices, there is often no conclusive answer. The best approach is to do some research, then get started in the way that looks most promising, reflecting as you go on whether tools are allowing you to achieve your goals. A certain amount of experimentation can lead to new ways of doing things that are beneficial, but it is also easy to get sucked in to regularly using new tools just because they are new and attractive in one way. Sometimes the investment of time in using something new could be better used to get the work done using your existing toolset.

For some people, however, the constant flux of tools can be a benefit. Experimentation with workflows and processes can reveal new ways of doing things, and even new possibilities for what can be achieved.

> I know people who get everything in their work environment just so, but current optimization is long-term anachronism. I'm in the business of weak signal detection, so at the end of every year, I junk a lot of perfectly good habits in favour of awkward new ones.
>
> (Clay Shirky, The Setup Interviews, 2014)

Such a sentiment really flies in the face of much of the advice contained in this chapter, and yet Shirky is clearly a highly productive writer of great influence. For some people, change and experimentation can be energizing, inspiring, and lead to new ways of working. Although Shirky's approach may seem potentially chaotic as described here, it's worth noting the mention that this is an annual ritual. Changing one's tools every time a new one comes along is unlikely to lead to productivity. However, there is an approach from agile software development that is a useful frame to this. Software developers use a 'sprint', a specific period of time to structure their work. At the start of a sprint, the requirements, goals, and tasks for the sprint are defined, and then they are 'locked down' and no changes can be made until the sprint is finished. This allows them to work productively towards a set of goals, taking the focused approach needed for programming tasks, similar to that needed for much academic work. At the end of the sprint they pause and review, reflect on whether they have reached the set goals, and allow a moment for changes in requirements to be taken account of and new plans made. Shirky describes something of an annual sprint in terms of his workflows and tools. A similar approach can be beneficial for achieving that balance of productive focus and openness to the fast changing nature of digital tools.

Just as long as the focus is on the work, and the tools as an enabler of this, then in this relatively new digital world, anything can go.

Conclusion

Changes in access to information, communication, and the tools available are all powerful influences on the practice of the modern academic. These changes rooted in technologies are giving rise to changes not just in how individuals work, but how researchers relate to one another, their research participants, the public, and almost any group that they engage with. So fast has the development of digital technology and digital culture been, that we are still working out how these relationships are changing and what effects they have.

The only thing that is constant is change.

— Heraclitus

One thing seems clear, for now, change will continue. Not only is the technology powering digital culture continuing to develop at a pace, the culture itself is built on a strong aesthetic of change. Researchers, as most other groups, have little choice than to build their agility in participating in digital culture. This chapter has argued that this is not a case of letting the digital world wash over you, with all of its distractions. A critical, focused approach is needed, focused on outcomes and yet enquiring as to the potentially unnoticed effects, the possibilities, and the drawbacks. This is the approach needed to be an effective digitally agile researcher, not such a departure from the time-tested core skills of any researcher. Turn your skills on the subject of your own digital engagement, and you will be on the way to making the most of what digital culture has to offer you.

Common Pitfalls

- Wallowing in information. Invest some time in organizing a reference management system and a workflow for reading, making notes, and storing papers and articles so you can find them in the future. Map out your information environment and consider where you get your information from and where else you might get it. Then prioritize, thinking carefully about how much information you can really handle.
- Over-indulging in communications. People are social beings and we love to discuss and share. However, academic work needs focus, so be sure to strike a good balance between communicating about the work and doing the work.
- Getting caught up with new tools. Investing time in exploring new possibilities and auditing your own workflows is well spent, but can become a never-ending process. Consider structuring it in 'sprints', where you use a particular workflow for some months or a particular project, then review and adapt or change at the end of this set period.

Best Practice

- Plan for what you want to get out of your digital engagement. It may be long term, and take several cycles to integrate everything into the way you work, but it's important to have a direction. As with all long-term plans, it is likely to flex and change as digital culture does, but if you have a direction you can make sound decisions about what to experiment with and adopt, and what to put aside.

- Think about the ultimate goal of your research and the difference you want it to make to people in the world. Understand that you can communicate with those people and others with similar goals at all stages in your process and learn from them, as they can learn from you. Transparency of academic work can have some challenges, but these are well worth working through for the relevance and the opportunities open communications can bring you.
- Strike a balance with your adoption of tools. Be open to genuinely new tools and approaches, but don't get caught up in trying every new tool and version that comes out if it draws you away from the core of your work. The digital world is built on distraction – the antithesis of successful academic work. Manage this well and you can gain great benefits from digital tools and not let them fuel procrastination.

References

Bohannon, J. (2016) The frustrated science student behind Sci-Hub, *Science*, 28 April [retrieved from: http://www.sciencemag.org/news/2016/04/alexandra-elbakyan-founded-sci-hub-thwart-journal-paywalls].

Goldacre, B. (2009) *Bad Science*. London: Harper Perennial.

Leadbeater, C. (2009) *We Think: Mass innovation, not mass production*. London: Profile Books.

The Setup Interviews (2014) *Clay Shirky* [retrieved from: https://usesthis.com/interviews/clay.shirky/].

Toffler, A. (1973) *Future Shock*. London: Pan Books.

Van Noorden, R. (2013) Open access: the true cost of science publishing, *Nature News*, 27 March [retrieved from: http://www.nature.com/news/open-access-the-true-cost-of-science-publishing-1.12676].

2

Open scholarship: leveraging social networks and communities as a digitally agile researcher

W. Ian O'Byrne

Introduction

A twenty-first-century educational system requires the effective and authentic use of the technologies that permeate society to prepare students for the future. In this context, researchers have little or no guidance on how to embed these new and digital literacies into their work process and product in open spaces. To prepare for and understand this future, researchers need opportunities not only to read but also write the 'web'. Despite the transformative possibilities associated with the inclusion of the internet and other communication technologies (ICTs) in instruction, relatively little is known about the regular use of these technologies in our daily lives. For researchers in particular, understanding how best to leverage these digital and web literacies in our work is central to our collective future.

In this chapter, I identify the knowledge, skills, and strategies that will help you act as a scholar and researcher in open, online spaces. I will discuss opportunities to use social network communities for research. This will require a focus on self-organizing, cross-functional work processes that adaptively plan, continuously improve, and are flexible to change. I will discuss these elements in the context of my own work, and a more collaborative project with other digitally agile researchers.

Three stages to build the habits

To develop the digitally agile approaches described here, you need to follow three steps on your own. My advice is first to develop your own personal 'cyber-infrastructure' (Campbell, 2009) and then allow others to join in the process through a collaborative project. Once you have the essential framework in place, you will attract attention and provide opportunities for others to join in, or follow the model that you have developed. In order to leverage and negotiate digital spaces, there are three stages that you will need to follow as you engage in open scholarship:

1   Create and curate your digital identity
2   Digitize your workflow
3   Build an online learning and research hub.

It is important to note that as you engage in open scholarship, you are exploring, examining, and creating online representations of your identity. In the post-Snowden era (Bajaj, 2014), there are also serious concerns about privacy and security online. The problem with this thinking is that by not creating and developing your own online brand, you are allowing others to do it for you. Not if, but when someone searches for you online, they'll only find information others have said about you. You should be the one to create and curate that information.

Create and curate your digital identity

The first step in this process is the need to create and curate your digital identity. Researchers spend a great deal of time preparing and polishing their identity in the 'real world'. We have a vision of who we are as individuals and ensure that our grooming habits, clothes, personas, and colleagues all mirror this vision. Most of the time, we pride ourselves on being organized and presenting ourselves in a positive light. Much of this veneer of professionalism and organization is not carried through to our digital identity.

Researchers may have a webpage on the school or organization website that shares personal and/or professional information. In addition, we may have social networks (Facebook, Twitter, LinkedIN, Google+) that are maintained or orphaned. These social networks typically contain the most up-to-date information about our works but they are infrequently connected to the website with our professional affiliations. There usually is little or no consistency in design or identity across these spaces. Finally, the identity presented across these spaces is usually inconsistent with the identity we present face-to-face. This is problematic given the fact that usually individuals search for information about us online before 'we meet face-to-face. You have to wonder what version of the 'truth' people are learning about you before you meet for the first time.

First steps: develop a picture of your identity

Think deeply about the identity you want to use to represent yourself online. Write down six words that capture exactly who you are, or who you would like to be. You should also identify the audience that you intend to reach, and the purpose for your interactions. Finally, what information will you share about yourself, and what will you keep private? What colours, images, and text will you use to build this identity? As an example, will you use a photo of yourself for your profile picture? I use an avatar that was developed by an eighth-grade student that was in one of my last classes I taught before beginning my doctoral work. I use this avatar to represent my online identity to ground myself of these experiences and to stick out a bit from the usual collection of selfies that people share online. You can keep all of this written down and refer back to it as you create and revise your identity across spaces. Once you have written these guidelines, go to each of your accounts for your various social networks and places that you appear online and edit the information they have about you. Keep it consistent. By keeping your design choices consistent across multiple spaces, you create a sense of professionalism and polish in your presented materials.

Digitize your workflow and processes

The second step in this process is to modify your workflow. Many of us have been indoctrinated into thinking that we have 'our office' and 'our computer' and that work only happens in these spaces as we create, manipulate, and save files on these machines. The problem is when you work from multiple locations, or when the computer crashes, your work is usually lost on that one computer. In a distributed, networked society, you need to be able to work from multiple places, and easily gain or provide access to all materials. This allows you to work from multiple locations and use multiple tools as you teach, present, or research. Your work and scholarship become ubiquitous as they follow you and are available when you need them.

To do this, you should develop a workflow that is device agnostic and allows ubiquitous access to data. Being device agnostic means that you can utilize any tool or platform at your disposal. This includes working on computers (Mac, PC, Linux), tablets (Android, iOS, Windows), or mobile devices (Android, iOS, Windows). Due to the influx of new technologies, you need to be adaptable and able to use any and all devices for research and scholarship. Having ubiquitous access to materials means that your work and materials are saved digitally and cloud-based. Having a cloud-based system to store and save all of your content creates opportunities to easily share with colleagues openly online. One of the challenges with this system is that you have to identify a work process that will maximize the instances that you are connected to the internet. You can create and revise your materials offline, but this requires an understanding and planning for these instances. There are many services that will allow you to build this system (Google Drive, DropBox, Windows Office, OwnCloud).

First steps: develop your workflow

Start by auditing your devices and current systems. Do you or your organization use Google Drive or Windows Office? What devices do you regularly use for work? Each of these cases will identify one platform that might be better than others for your situation. For example, if you use a Chromebook for work, Google Drive might be the best option for you. Once you have identified a system that works best for the devices and systems, start by creating only cloud-based versions of new materials. This means that if you are developing a PowerPoint for use in a lecture or demonstration, you should create it in Google Slides or a comparable product. If you're writing a paper or developing a syllabus, this should live as a Google Doc. There are opportunities to digitize all of your old materials, but I advise against this. I would start this process by building all new content using these cloud-based tools. As you identify older content that you'll need, you can convert this as needed. Through the creation and use of digital texts, you create more opportunities to easily share your work process and product online.

Build a hub for your digital identity

The final step in this process is the need to build and establish an online learning hub. As you create and curate your online brand, your identity will be spread across numerous spaces online. Many of these online social networks act as silos and only privilege their content. As an example, Google, Twitter, and Facebook frequently change the access to your data that they provide to each other. The end result is that your great work on your Facebook or Twitter profile might not be accessible when someone 'Googles' you.

You should also consider what happens when you meet someone for the first time, or they happen to come across some part of your digital identity. How much are they learning about you if they only read some of your recent tweets? Is that an adequate or complete picture of you? If you build and maintain one space on the internet, you can archive and/or share materials using your own website. This allows colleagues and friends the opportunity to look back through the digital breadcrumbs that you have left online to get a more complete picture of you.

First steps: develop your online hub

There are many options when building up and iterating on your online learning hub. I would suggest using one of the free services available while you start building up your website. WordPress is an excellent example of a tool that is open sourced and will allow you to easily move from their free option [https://wordpress.com/] to a self-hosted version [https://wordpress.org/]. As you plan and build your website, remember that this is primarily for documenting, archiving, and sharing content. I believe any of the options listed above are a good starting point to build up a domain of your own (O'Byrne and Pytash, 2017). As you plan, build, and revise your website, you can then consider the URL (address) for your website and ensure that all of these elements are connected across online spaces.

My experiences with open scholarship

My research investigates the literacy practices of individuals as they read, write, and communicate in online or hybrid spaces. In this, I believe the internet and the new associated literacy practices are changing the ways in which we engage in scholarship, research, and develop our identities. As a researcher, especially in digital spaces, I believe it is important that we allow these texts to inform the ways in which we present our identities. One opportunity that exists involves encouraging researchers to openly learn and engage in social scholarship practices. Social scholarship utilizes ICTs to evolve the ways in which scholarship is conducted (Greenhow et al., 2009). Social scholarship as a process is designed to connect formal scholarship with informal, social internet-based civic practices while embodying specific values, such as openness, collaboration, transparency, access, and sharing (Ellison, 2007; Greenhow, 2009; Lankshear and Knobel, 2011).

Web-literate researchers need to recognize and use these social media texts as readers and writers in online spaces (O'Byrne, 2014). The internet should profoundly affect scholarly relations because research and scholarship should not be silent, solitary, or ruminative (Kessler, 2000). Social scholarship promotes an educational identity and purpose, while stimulating discussion of theory and pedagogy (North, 2006; Greenhow et al., 2009). Ideas are ultimately transmitted more quickly and innovatively than in formal journals and channels that may be constrained by issues of publication, access, and location.

As digitally agile researchers, the opportunity exists to use a variety of digital spaces and digital tools to create and curate our digital identities. We can create and host our own websites to hold our research materials, notes, and reflections. We can use social media to tweet, blog, and post about research and important events in the field. These platforms could and should be linked to other scholarly websites that allow us to maintain and build our professional digital identities. These varied platforms and connections exist in the online collaborative space as we act as networked, social scholars (Greenhow, 2009; Wise and O'Byrne, 2015). As detailed previously, I strive for a workflow that is device agnostic and allows me ubiquitous access to my materials.

Examining my workflow

I use a series of digital texts and tools to build and maintain my profile and identity as a digital researcher. The linchpin of this system is my main website that acts as a hub for all of these connections. My hub is a WordPress site that I pay to host my own domain. This is important as the URL, identity, and all content remain online as long as I continue to pay for hosting. By paying for your own hosting of a website, you never have to worry about it being taken down or being discontinued by the company that hosts it.

I use this website to archive and share my research publications, links to all projects, and most importantly, blog about my work. This process of reflectively blogging and openly synthesizing is important, as I use it to synthesize and share my work quickly with my audience. I frequently share drafts of articles or chapters with colleagues for feedback, or share researcher notes to document my thinking openly online. Using my blog to openly reflect and share online adds to the level of audience and authenticity with which I attend to my work.

Everything that I create and share is usually in Google Drive. I use Google Docs for writing and planning. I use Google Slides for all of my presentations. I use Google Forms and Spreadsheets for assessments in classes and during research. I do have some concern about using one provider (e.g. Google) to handle all of my materials and I am currently exploring the use of free and open source materials to better control my own materials. These are usually the tools that we use to create and share teaching, learning, and research materials. Sharing your materials openly online has the potential to raise the level of credibility and validity of your work as you make it accessible for review to alleviate threats to validity in your work. From my own experience, I regularly receive feedback on my writing and research by sharing these documents with critical friends to obtain their input.

Audio and video are also a large part of my toolset as I work, research, and interact online. Most video involves recording interviews and conducting meetings online using video conferencing software. These videos are shared openly online at YouTube to allow anyone to review and respond to the content. Audio content usually consists of researcher notes, or audio ripped from the videos and shared to make it easier for individuals to consume on mobile devices. Audio content can be saved and shared using the free hosting provided by the Internet Archive [https://archive.org/index.php]. The purpose of sharing these materials openly online allows anyone to easily consume and utilize them if they so choose.

I use social networks in my work primarily as a communication and platform for dissemination of work. I use my website and collections of audio and video content to create a pipeline of information that I share openly online. Specifically, I subscribe to the POSSE [Publish (on your) Own Site, Syndicate Elsewhere] model when sharing and connecting online. This means that I post all content to my site and use social networks to drive eyes to my work on my site. I use various open source plugins on my site to ensure that comments and discussion on the various social networks I use (Twitter, Facebook, Google+, LinkedIN) are documented and archived on the post on my website. I use a free service called Bridgy [https://brid.gy/] that automatically archives these comments on my website. Put simply, I am looking for some unity and organization in what I share online. All links and social network connections link back to my content on my website.

Example from practice: The WalkMyWorld Project

In the elements that I have detailed up until this point, I have described most of the work that I do individually, which allows me to create and curate my online identity as a researcher. One of the advantages of building in the philosophies and tools identified herein is that it is quickly adaptable for use in working collaboratively on research projects with colleagues. This focus on reflecting, sharing, and communicating in the open during a research project also provides opportunities to develop secondary or tertiary meta-analyses in which other scholars may review your work, results, or replicate the methods and procedures shared. I believe that there is an opportunity and a need to allow scholars across global spaces with the raw materials and know-how to build a global resource fuelled by research in digital spaces.

As an example of these opportunities, I focus on a collaborative research project that I have helped facilitate and that unites researchers with educators and students from pre-kindergarten up through higher education. The #WalkMyWorld project was a social media experiment developed to provide pre-service teachers, veteran teachers, and K-12 (the final year before college) students with an opportunity to develop media literacies and civic engagement in online spaces. Participants were encouraged to engage in online social scholarship to discover how social media and networking could be integrated into classroom instructional routines. This collaborative research project yielded a series of publications for the researchers involved (McVerry et al., 2015; Pytash et al., 2015; Rish and Pytash, 2015; Wise and O'Byrne, 2015). The project was self-funded and ran from 2014 to 2016. For more information about the #WalkMyWorld Project, please visit http://walkmy.world/.

During each iteration of the study, the participants shared images, videos, and writing on Twitter using the hashtag #WalkMyWorld for the weeks. The hashtag was framed as an invitation to create and to collaborate in online spaces and, in doing so, to allow others to 'walk in your world'. The project allowed educators to engage in the process of multimodal meaning-making with various digital texts and tools. Participants worked openly online to create a community of inquiry exploring uses of social media as a tool for focusing on media literacies (Garrison et al., 2006). In this work, educators manipulated and remixed digital content within a social and connected learning environment.

It is important to remember that this example of a massive open online course (MOOC) was developed by educators and for educators. These practices require a broadened definition of 'text' and that we research how exemplary teaching and learning manifest in online communities and hybrid spaces (Pytash and O'Byrne, 2014). As such, the #WalkMyWorld Project was conceived as a third space to support learners in online spaces, offering a new organizational structure within face-to-face undergraduate- and graduate-level education courses.

Although #WalkMyWorld invited participants from across the globe and from various other instructional settings, this open educational resource centred on teacher educators from various institutions of higher education chaperoning pre-service and in-service teachers as they interacted in online spaces. It provided a space not only for researchers to consider the affordances of new technologies, sprawling online spaces, and spiralling social network communities, but also to simultaneously reflect upon these in relation to the foundational tenets of education. As such, the project shed light on the potential advantages of our adaptation of the familiar MOOC and digital spaces as an educational enterprise.

At this point, the #WalkMyWorld Project has evolved through three iterations, that is, three sets of ten learning events over the course of three years. Year one participants initially included professors, teachers, pre-service teachers, and adolescents identified by a core group of researchers in the USA. Ultimately, it attracted the curiosity of participants from schools and universities across the country and the globe, many of whom became repeat participants and/or mentors during year two. In the second year of the project, the ten learning events focused on creating and curating a digital identity for use in teaching and learning. In the third year of the project, the ten learning events expanded this examination of digital identity as participants worked not only to read, but also write the web. This meant that they became not only consumers but also active and proactive participants in the online space.

Common Pitfalls

- To alleviate concerns about not having the time or resources to work through these stages, keep in mind that your focus should be on working differently, not working harder.
- Be wary of the challenges in open scholarship as we explore new models of research and publishing. You should routinely re-examine issues of validity, reliability, and ethics in your research.
- Understand that there are current challenges and concerns about being a 'public intellectual' online. You will have to learn to advocate for yourself and the role of this work in the field.

Best Practice

- Start small by developing written plans and site maps to plan your personal cyber-infrastructure. Regularly refer back to the paper documents when the digital spaces become complex.
- Begin creating and integrating digital content over time. Archive older materials and share as needed.
- Regularly audit and iterate on the process and revise personal cyber-infrastructure as needed.

Cited resources

Bridgy [https://brid.gy/]
DropBox [https://www.dropbox.com/]
Facebook [https://www.facebook.com/]
Google+ [https://plus.google.com/]
Google Drive [https://www.google.com/drive/]
Internet Archive [https://archive.org/index.php]
LinkedIN [https://www.linkedin.com/]
OwnCloud [https://owncloud.org/]

POSSE model [https://indieweb.org/POSSE]
#WalkMyWorld Project [http://walkmy.world/]
Windows Office [https://www.office.com/]
WordPress (Free option) [https://wordpress.com/]
WordPress (Self hosted) [https://wordpress.org/]

References

Bajaj, K. (2014) Cyberspace: post-Snowden, *Strategic Analysis*, 38 (4): 582–587.

Campbell, G. (2009) A personal cyberinfrastructure, *Educause Review*, 44 (5): 58–59.

Ellison, N.B. (2007) Social network sites: definition, history, and scholarship, *Journal of Computer-Mediated Communication*, 13 (1): 210–230.

Garrison, D.R., Kanuka, H. and Hawes, D. (2006) *Communities of inquiry* [retrieved from: http://commons.ucalgary.ca/documents/Comm_of_Inquiry.pdf; accessed 1 May 2006]. University of Calgary, Alberta: Learning Commons.

Greenhow, C. (2009) Tapping the wealth of social networks for professional development, *Learning & Leading with Technology*, 36 (8): 10–11.

Greenhow, C., Robelia, B. and Hughes, J.E. (2009) Learning, teaching, and scholarship in a digital age: Web 2.0 and classroom research: what path should we take now?, *Educational Researcher*, 38 (4): 246–259.

Kessler, R. (2000) *The Soul of Education: Helping students find connection, compassion, and character at school*. Alexandria, VA: ASCD.

Lankshear, C. and Knobel, M. (2011) *New Literacies*. Maidenhead: McGraw-Hill Education.

McVerry, G., O'Byrne, I., Pytash, K., Rish, R.M., Shields, M. and Wise, J. (2015) The #WalkMyWorld Project, in E. Gordon and P. Milhailidis (eds) *Civic Media Project*. Cambridge, MA: MIT Press [retrieved from: https://sites.google.com/site/walkmyworldproject/].

North, C.E. (2006) More than words? Delving into the substantive meaning(s) of 'social justice' in education, *Review of Educational Research*, 76 (4): 507–535.

O'Byrne, W.I. (2014) Empowering learners in the reader/writer nature of the digital informational space, *Journal of Adolescent & Adult Literacy*, 58 (2): 102–104.

O'Byrne, W.I. and Pytash, K.E. (2017) Becoming literate digitally in a digitally literate environment of their own, *Journal of Adolescent & Adult Literacy*, 60 (5): 499–504.

Pytash, K.E. and O'Byrne, W.I. (2014) Research on literacy instruction and learning in virtual, blended and hybrid environments, in R. Ferdig and K. Kennedy (eds) *Handbook of Research on K-12 Online and Blended Learning* (pp. 179–200). Pittsburgh, PA: ETC Press.

Pytash, K.E., Testa, E. and Nigh, J. (2015) Writing the world: preservice teachers' perceptions of 21st century writing instruction, *Teaching/Writing: The Journal of Writing Teacher Education*, 4 (1): 8.

Rish, R.M. and Pytash, K.E. (2015) Kindling the pedagogic imagination: preservice teachers writing with social media, *Voices from the Middle*, 23 (2): 37.

Wise, J.B. and O'Byrne, W.I. (2015) Social scholars educators' digital identity construction in open, online learning environments, *Literacy Research: Theory, Method, and Practice*, 64 (1): 398–414.

3

Using social media for action research: the benefits and limitations

Steve Wheeler

Introduction

Social media is a relatively new phenomenon, but it has already become an important part of academic life (Gruzd et al., 2012). How can you use social media for research? In this chapter, I explore ways this can be achieved. But before this, a brief examination of social media is necessary.

Social media first emerged as a part of the evolution of the internet known as the social web, or Web 2.0 (O'Reilly, 2005). As the web developed into a more participatory medium, so tools and services emerged to facilitate the increased demand for social engagement. Social media can be variously classified into social networks (e.g. Facebook, WhatsApp), photo sharing tools (Flickr, Instagram, Snapchat), video sharing tools (Vimeo, YouTube), social bookmarking sites (Delicious, Diigo), aggregation and curation tools (Pinterest, Scoop.it), and blogging services (Wordpress, Blogger, Tumblr). This list of tools is not exhaustive.

In the last decade, Microblogging services such as Twitter have also emerged as popular tools that create meeting points for social exchange. These tools have become increasingly popular because they provide users with digital spaces within which to share experiences, ideas and artefacts, while celebrating, informing and discussing in a rich social milieu (Wheeler, 2015). Here, I explore some of the affordances and constraints of social media when they are used as data-gathering tools. The word 'data' in this context is not solely defined as information or 'facts', but in a wider and broader sense can also refer to the opinions of individuals or groups, and can take on various forms including textual, audio, visual, and other formats. For the purposes of this chapter, I will examine the ways social media can be used to support action research.

Rationale and justification

In a piece of action research, you will likely try to address a question or challenge that has arisen through your reflection on previous experience or practice, and then try to effect some change. Questions can be formulated into research questions, which then act as drivers for the entire research process, including your choice of data-gathering methods, data analysis and interpretation. A good research question can also undergird and inform theoretical development and methodological considerations.

Choosing social media as a means to garner research data is a specific choice you can make when you wish to gain a perspective on questions that may be grounded in, but not exclusively determined by, the use of digital media and technology. Given that many work-based practices, particularly those within professions, rely heavily on the use of networked and connected tools and technologies, it would seem appropriate that social media could be used with clear justification as data-gathering tools. Social media also provide a rich source of naturally occurring data, which often relate directly to the lives and experiences of those who generate them.

Crowdsourcing

One of the recent trends to emerge from social media proliferation has been the practice of crowdsourcing. This practice involves the gathering of views and responses from networks of people to ascertain what might be a dominant viewpoint. Social media are ideal tools to perform this kind of data gathering, because they are the platforms on which potential participants perform their lives and share their content and views. Twitter, for example, can be a rich source of data that crystallize over a period of time when people enter into a discourse around their own interests, communities of practice or professional engagement. Groups can make decisions that are often sound, in a process that relies on the 'wisdom of crowds' principle described by Surowiecki (2009), who argues that, in most cases, large groups of people are smarter than a few experts. While this is seen as problematic by some commentators (for example, Keen, 2007), it is a largely fallacious argument. In Wikipedia, for example, content over time becomes more accurate due to the constant editing and revision of interested parties. As Tapscott and Williams (2008) argue, when people collaborate en masse, surprising advances occur in the arts, science and education.

The principle of crowdsourcing has already been used in research that pre-dates social media and the internet. Discussion forums, questionnaire surveys, and focus groups are tried-and-trusted research methods that gain access to the shared thoughts and prevailing values of groups of individuals, when they are faced with the same question or challenge. It follows that the digital version of such methods can be applied within the large and almost limitless expression of group views that can be found in social media.

Data mining

Many organizations are now practising sentiment tracking, which is the data mining of specific phrases or key words that represent the emotions and feelings of people towards a particular product, service or event. The ability to discover the views of customers or potential clients can be invaluable for many businesses in the shaping and marketing of their services and products. A key value is the immediacy and personalization that companies can apply when addressing specific concerns for individuals.

I once arrived for an important speech in a foreign country only to discover that my suitcase (with my suit, shoes, toiletries, and other essential personal effects) has been stranded at another airport. The airline officials apologized for the inconvenience and promised me that my bags would arrive at my hotel on the next available flight – which just happened to be the following day. I was due to speak the following morning, so I wasn't particularly impressed by this news.

When I arrived at my hotel, I expressed my annoyance on Twitter, naming the airline and the predicament in which I found myself. Within an hour, the airline representative responded to my tweet with a public apology and a pledge that whatever I needed to purchase to replace the lost items would be reimbursed promptly. This is an example of sentiment tracking that is not only good customer relations (I was more inclined to use the services of the airline in the future) but also something that could be used by researchers who are interested in specific trends.

In the context of this chapter, we can extend sentiment tracking further, using the principles of social media data mining, to many kinds of research. One recently applied technique employs sentiment tracking of social network status updates, which are then plotted onto a geomapping tool to indicate the 'hot spots' that are emerging in various parts of a city, region or country. Such techniques can be used to predict mass civil unrest, the progress of social movements, or even the outbreak of a virus or epidemic. Known as techno-social predictive analysis (TPA), this technique has much promise if you wish to do some wider analysis of social data, especially that of an emotive or affective nature (Kamel Boulos et al., 2010). For large-scale sampling, across a wide geographical area, this may be a viable research method you wish to employ.

Research dialogues

The term research dialogue can be used to describe data that are gathered through interaction or as a dialogue with peers about research. Later in the chapter I will discuss the latter, but here we focus on the former.

Most interviews are conducted face-to-face, within a co-located environment. However, it is increasingly likely, with the proliferation of digital technologies, that a community of interest will be geographically distributed. In such circumstances, you are likely to conduct your interviews using video and audio services such as Skype. Adopting this approach to synchronous technology-mediated conversations meets the need for interviews to be as full and rich a social encounter as possible (Cohen et al., 2007).

One specific approach to research in social media is the research dialogue. Researchers can facilitate such a dialogue in an online discussion with groups or individuals. Dialogue is usually free-flowing and therefore unstructured, but the catalyst for such dialogue can be a series of structured questions or prompts, as seen in Twitter discussions such as #Edchat and #EDENchat. Although these online discussions are not specifically focused on the generation of research data, there is potential for them to be applied as such. Not only are research dialogues intrinsically valuable, they can also open up new avenues of enquiry that you might otherwise have missed.

Personally, I have entered into research dialogues with readers of my blog, and also on Twitter, to discuss relevant issues that can later be written up as research narratives. Clearly, there are issues of authenticity and reliability here (see an extended discussion of this later in the chapter) but in general it must be accepted that the very nature of social media-generated data tends to be messy and unpredictable. Researchers should also bear in mind that the development of research dialogues online can extend into days or even weeks as the asynchronous nature of Twitter and other social media plays out. They should also consider that the direction of a dialogue can alter unpredictably depending on the nature of the topic, who is online at the time, and the individual views and perceptions of each respondent.

Secondary data

Primary data are data that are generated through the efforts of the researcher. These can come in qualitative or quantitative formats. However, an area of data that is often largely overlooked is secondary data – data generated by others that can be accessed and used by third parties for research purposes. A commonly used source of secondary data is literature. Researchers often use previously published literature, data generated by others, and artefacts that can be repurposed for research purposes. One of the major sources of secondary data in the digital age is the large repositories of text, images, and other artefacts created and shared by social media users. Known as user-generated content, these sources are often overlooked by researchers, but can offer you a rich vein of information that is relevant to just about any research question, if you know where to look and how to search effectively.

Locating online content by using search engines such as Google is the dominant practice of most researchers and scholars. Selecting the correct term or phrase can yield good results, but more often than not, may just as easily lead the seeker down many blind alleyways with little to show for their efforts. To find quality secondary data, you should try to be as specific as possible, and you would be advised to learn and use techniques such as Boolean operators (+, –, AND, NOT) and 'parentheses' [i.e. ()] to eliminate spurious content and isolate the specific content you are seeking.

An alternative to the search engine is the computational knowledge engine. A prime example of this is Wolfram Alpha, which can be used to discover content through asking direct questions of the database. Wolfram Alpha also isolates related content. It is easy on standard search engines such as Google, for example, to find content related to 'Tony Blair' or the 'Fall of the Berlin Wall'. It is not so easy to ascertain specific facts such as 'How old was Tony Blair when the Berlin Wall fell?' When asked this specific question, Wolfram Alpha will return with the answer '36 years, 6 months and 3 days'.

A rich source of secondary qualitative data can be found on blogs and other predominantly text-based repositories such as wikis. Blogs are usually written by individuals wishing to share their content and ideas with a larger audience, with the content often based upon a specific topic or speciality. Some blogs are run by a small group or community of contributors, as is the case with many wikis. You can easily check the content of these sites to determine whether it is reusable and copyright-free.

Often bloggers include a Creative Commons (CC) logo to content which indicates to the reader which user licence has been applied. Your prime consideration for ethical use of such content is that the source should always be acknowledged, and that subsequent sharing and use of the content should perpetuate the original CC licence. The 'rule of thumb' is that if a CC licence is not evident, then by default the work is copyrighted. If you are in doubt as to the copyright status of any content you discover, you should either avoid using it or politely approach the owner of the content to obtain permission. It is also worth noting that many scholars are now citing blog posts and other online texts in the same manner as they would cite scientific articles. The former falls into the category of 'grey literature' because it has not been through the same formal process of peer review as 'white literature'.

Examples using social media for research

On several occasions, students have come to me with the problem that while attempting to gather data with questionnaires, no one is responding to their requests. This is understandable when so many people are extremely busy and are reluctant to respond to paper-based surveys that arrive suddenly through their letterboxes. A similar situation arises when they receive requests through e-mail. On such occasions, I have advised my students to tap into the huge well of data that are available on social media platforms. Those who are likely to respond will be online because they wish to be and are sometimes more amenable to requests. Furthermore, as Shirky (2010) argues, now that social media has made sharing easier and afforded permanence, people are more likely to give of their time freely, especially if they perceive a benefit for the entire community. The technique involves posting a link on a widely used service such as Twitter or Facebook, with the incorporation of an online survey tool such as Survey Monkey, Zoho or Esurveycreator at the end of the link. All of the tools mentioned are free to students, and all can be adapted to meet the needs of the researcher.

There are some restrictions – for example, the current free version of Survey Monkey restricts users to ten questions and limited data analysis tools. However, with some workarounds, students have successfully used this combination of tools to gather large amounts of data that can be analysed and presented in their research projects.

Limitations and constraints

Validity

Each affordance is countered with a constraint. When using social media to gather research data, one of the key constraints is that the responses will have a specific bias. Everyone who responds to questionnaires on Twitter or other social media is clearly going to be a user of the technology. This means that only technology users are represented in the sample, while non-technology users are excluded. As long as this limitation is acknowledged, however, and the method is justified, the research can be viewed as having ecological validity. A further issue is that it is difficult for the researcher to ascertain whether respondents are who they claim to be. If my students are researching the views of teachers (or parents), for example, what checks and balances can they put in place to ensure that only teachers (or parents) respond to the questions?

The answer is, of course, that they can't. Researchers can devise question items within their survey that attempt to weed out imposters, but in general they are at the mercy of the problem. Once again, as long as this limitation is acknowledged and engaged with critically, the research method may be deemed valid.

Reliability

Perhaps the most difficult challenge for online investigators is the issue of the reliability of data collected online. The potential for multiple submission or responses from single individuals must be acknowledged. Clearly, such an eventuality would contaminate and invalidate the data obtained, causing skewed results. To limit this possibility, you should employ digital means to limit multiple responses. This is normally a simple click of a button, which prevents respondents from intentionally or inadvertently pressing the send button more than once. Although it is a simple solution, it is one that is often overlooked by new researchers, an error that can cause significant problems during later data analysis.

Some researchers have expressed concerns that people behave differently online compared with 'real life', which may cause data to be unreliable (Benninger et al., 2014). While being online affords anonymity and can promote free speaking, it can also distort reality, leading to an increased possibility for some respondents to be dishonest or exaggerate their responses. Clearly, these are challenges that are not unique to online environments, but they are nevertheless issues that researchers need to be aware of when they use social media as data-gathering tools. However, if you intend to investigate specific human traits such as online behaviour, data gathered through social media are more likely to be representative of human behaviour or views than data gathered in 'real life'. You should be aware of, and consider the issues of, authentic responses and reliability, regardless of the area you are exploring.

Amplifying content

It is imperative that researchers who wish to disseminate their work through social media find ways to amplify their content. Posting a link or publishing research in a blog is often not enough to guarantee wider readership. Amplification of content can only be achieved when a sufficient critical mass of potential readers is within a network. Some individuals and small groups of academics enjoy high subscriber numbers of more than 10,000 on Twitter, for example. If a researcher is able to enlist the support of influential Twitter users, their work can be amplified across a larger network of potential users, who in turn may re-tweet links onwards, if they find them useful. The art of content amplification on Twitter is being able to identify and connect with users who are influential, and post content that is of sufficiently high quality for them to wish to share it further within their networks.

Communicating with the community

For centuries, the traditional route for research dissemination has been the peer-reviewed journal and conference paper presentations. The former is still highly prized as the prime route for publishing empirical findings to the professional community, while the latter can be prestigious, depending on the status of the conference. In recent years, however, with the rise in popularity of the internet and social media, new and alternative routes of dissemination have emerged. Although these alternative routes are not yet as highly valued by the professional and academic communities, dissemination of research through blogging, open access online journals, webinars, and other non-conventional routes is gaining traction.

Academic blogging has proliferated in recent years, but is usually the preserve of academics who are *au fait* with the power and utility of the social web. Increasing amounts of academic content are published online, often as serialized parts of a journal article, or as entire papers, or as redacted versions, for public information. Some sites are highly respected, due mainly to the reputations of the academics who contribute.

Some academics are also discovering that publishing their books online, in open access format, can gain them substantially larger audiences. Those who practise academic blogging usually claim that they gain wider readership for their work than if they simply published their findings in closed, peer-reviewed journals, which traditionally enjoy exclusive, limited readership. For similar reasons, many academics are turning to open access journals as a major method of dissemination. Again, the claim is that a larger audience can be secured compared with traditional closed journals. There is also a moral argument, resulting from the practice of traditional closed journal publishers to charge for publicly funded research, while expecting academics to work as editors, reviewers, and authors for free.

Perhaps the most valuable aspect of engaging with social media for the sharing of research is the affordance of dialogue. Research dialogue, in this sense, goes beyond data gathering to the point where academics and scholars can engage in free-flowing and unlimited discussion around theories and practice, and can learn from each other, regardless of geographical or temporal constraints. Whether dialogue occurs at the core of the community of practice or at the periphery, it can be seen as legitimate, because by engaging in the process of active discussion or observation of the discussion through the social media, all participants have the potential to learn and reify their membership of their community (Lave and Wenger, 1991). Situated learning of this nature has intrinsic value for the individual, and extrinsic value for the entire community. Access to an archive of the interactions can further amplify ideas around the wider community and thus increase social and cultural capital (Bourdieu and Passeron, 1990).

Conclusion

In the digital age, social media have become an important component in the research equation. For both gathering data and for dissemination of research, use of the social web offers researchers a very powerful set of tools to engage with the wider research community, and the public in general. There is a wealth of naturally occurring data in social media, and the widespread use of services also provides a large audience. Specific uses of the social web have already yielded important and valuable rewards for academics. Engaging with others on social media can yield naturalistic and ecologically valid data, and it can also prompt rich and meaningful research dialogues that benefit the entire professional community while opening up new avenues of enquiry.

Activities

1 Search for education and research chats on Twitter. Follow a few and see what you can learn from your online community of practice. Examples include #EdChat, #LTHEChat, #EDENchat, and #ResearchChat.
2 Use the Google advanced search function to find copyright-free images. Go to image search and drop down the Tools menu. Select 'Usages Rights' and then look for the CC licence on the images you see.
3 What are the ethical implications of crowdsourcing your data using social media?
4 What issues will you need to consider when gathering data from an anonymous source via social media?
5 List peer-reviewed sources (white literature) and non-peer-reviewed sources (grey literature). How can each be used in a research report?

Common Pitfalls

- Social media is a rich source, but brings its own considerations in terms of ethics, reliability and validity. What are the ethical implications of crowdsourcing your data using social media? What issues will you need to consider when gathering data from an anonymous source via social media?
- The web provides access to unprecedented amounts of information, allowing researchers to look well beyond the peer-reviewed literature, but this brings the need to carefully consider how different sources are used. Both peer-reviewed sources (white literature) and non-peer-reviewed sources (grey literature) are useful, but they should not be relied upon in the same way, so consider their uses carefully.

Best Practice

- Search for education and research chats on Twitter. Follow a few and see what you can learn from your online community of practice. Examples include #EdChat, #LTHEChat, #EDENchat and #ResearchChat.
- Use the Google advanced search function to find copyright free images. Go to image search and drop down the Tools menu. Select 'Usages Rights' and then look for the CC licence on the images you see.

References

Benninger, K., Fry, A., Jago, N., Lepps, H., Nass, L. and Sylvester, H. (2014) Research using social media: users' views. London: NatCen Social Research [retrieved from: http://www.natcen.ac.uk/media/282288/p0639-research-using-social-media-report-final-190214.pdf; accessed 26 August 2016].

Bourdieu, P. and Passeron, J.C. (1990) *Reproduction in Education, Society and Culture.* London: Sage.

Cohen, L., Manion, L. and Morrison, K. (2007) *Research Methods in Education.* London: Routledge.

Gruzd, A., Staves, K. and Wilk, A. (2012) Connected scholars: examining the role of social media in research practices of faculty using the UTAUT model, *Computers in Human Behaviour,* 28 (6): 2340–2350.

Kamel Boulos, M.N., Sanfilippo, A.P., Corley, C.D. and Wheeler, S. (2010) Social web mining and exploitation for serious applications: Technosocial Predictive Analysis and related technologies for public health, environmental and national security surveillance, *Computer Methods and Programs in Biomedicine,* 100 (1): 16–23.

Keen, A. (2007) *The Cult of the Amateur: How today's Internet is killing our culture and assaulting our economy.* London: Nicholas Brealey.

Lave, J. and Wenger, E. (1991) *Situated Learning: Legitimate peripheral participation.* Cambridge: Cambridge University Press.

O'Reilly, T. (2005) What is Web 2.0?, O'Reilly.com [retrieved from: http://www.oreilly.com/pub/a/web2/archive/what-is-web-20.html; accessed 26 August 2016].

Shirky, C. (2010) *Cognitive Surplus: Creativity and generosity in a connected age.* London: Penguin.

Surowiecki, J. (2009) *The Wisdom of Crowds: Why the many are smarter than the few.* London: Abacus.

Tapscott, D. and Williams, A. (2008) *Wikinomics: How mass collaboration changes everything.* London: Atlantic Books.

Wheeler, S. (2015) *Learning with 'e's: Educational theory and practice in the digital age.* Carmarthen: Crown House.

4

Academic blogging

Carl Gombrich

Introduction

Blogging platforms afford space for aggregating recent and important issues from diverse contexts and settings. Blogs can be written by well-established as well as emerging scholars across institutions. In addition, and unlike academic publications, blogs enable dissemination and public engagement on an open access and dynamic platform. What are the advantages of joining a well-established blogging platform over running your own blogging site? What are the common obstacles and common mistakes academic bloggers make? What is the kind of language readers are looking for and how can you correctly embed links in your posts? And most importantly, is blogging worth the time investment? In this chapter, I share some insights from fellow bloggers and my own blogging practice of the past five years.

It is challenging to say anything about the internet that does not date quickly. No doubt many of us have our favourite internet commentators and futurologists (mine include David Weinberger and Jaron Lanier), those contemporary seers who seem both to grasp the present better and to see the future more accurately and in more detail than the rest of us. But for the more usual academic teacher or scholar of a different field, the swings and unexpected turnings of the digital revolution can catch them completely unaware and require them to pivot quickly in their learning, teaching and wider thinking. How many academics were seriously considering the impact of 'fake news' and 'post-truth' on politics, economics, and possibly the entire university system and the livelihoods of academics within it just one year ago?

Faced with such historic challenges, it may be tempting to retreat to familiar ivory towers and fall back on pre-internet ways of doing things. But this would be a mistake: few academics long for the return of scholasticism and a cloistering of universities from the outside world. And although it is a misused word, most academics would like their work to be 'relevant' in some important way.

So, it is with caution yet some sense of urgency that I approach the subject of 'academic blogging'. If we manage to reflect this moment faithfully, then anything written on the subject will be just that: a faithful reflection of the moment – which in itself is a worthwhile achievement. For a subject like academic blogging, I think this is a more realistic approach than trying to be too neutral or objective, or trying to achieve any kind of 'universal'. I honestly have no idea whether much academic blogging will exist in five years' time. Perhaps blogging and other forms of social media will have exploded and become the main means of dissemination for a new generation of academics. But there is another scenario that is at least as likely: apart from the more generic surprises that this knowledge revolution throws up, the way the web is moving to an app-based phenomenon (and all the horror of filter bubbles that this implies) means that we may see the next generation not connecting through the world wide web in the way we anticipated roughly between 2000 and 2012. In this case, much of what I say here about blogging may become irrelevant. Even so – to repeat – this chapter would still serve as a small testament to how things were for this period. Correspondingly, an attempt is made in the conclusion of this chapter to capture, in a more vivid style, the urgency of the debates and dilemmas that arise from these considerations.

A blogging narrative

Blogging, vlogging, and social media, especially Twitter, have been absolutely central to my development as an academic. However, my career trajectory is atypical so I would like to share some biography and interweave it with reflections on the role of blogging and new media in academic careers. There are umpteen excellent blogs about blogging out there – including some good blogs on academic blogging (LSE, 2017) – and I am unlikely to improve on these here. Rather, I will share my personal blogging journey as one way to make sense of the particular role blogging and social media have played for me. I hope this will allow the reader to work out what to take from my experience and how best to apply it to their own circumstances.

The structure of this chapter will therefore be somewhat chronological, although I address the following themes:

- getting started
- playing and experimenting
- technicalities
- aspects of style
- forming networks
- connections with more traditional academic work
- strategy and time investment
- challenges and recognition
- future developments.

Key sentences and take-homes are italicized.

Background

I came to what you might call 'academia proper' only six years ago, in my mid-forties when I was appointed Programme Director of UCL's interdisciplinary liberal Arts and Sciences BASc degrees. Before that, I had a smaller and more administrative job within UCL running the international foundation programmes. And before that I was a teacher of physics on the same programmes, and before that an opera singer . . .

The Arts and Sciences BASc degrees are, in the UK context at least, highly innovative interdisciplinary undergraduate programmes. There are more closely related degrees in the USA and Australia, but in the UK – the land of the Two Cultures – the idea that students can span and synthesize different disciplines at undergraduate level is still not widely accepted, let alone implemented in university curricula (Snow, 1993). The conceptual, intellectual, practical, administrative and leadership demands of developing and leading the BASc are great, but the project has been a success, with an intake of 120 students per year, excellent graduate outcomes, and a significant national and international profile.

Getting started with blogging: the importance of play, experimentation and thinking out loud

In a sense, I had no 'right' to be given the job to lead the development and establishment of such a high-profile innovation. For example, although I had achieved degrees in maths and physics to master's level in my twenties, and more recently an MA in philosophy, I had never taken a PhD. However, I was successful at interview and at once was inspired to succeed on such an exciting and important project. Lacking the usual networks and career structure of a 'normal' academic, blogging and new media presented themselves as a vital way to develop my thoughts and to experiment – both with ideas themselves and with new forms of presenting these ideas.

I needed a place to play and try things out, and I didn't mind if this was public. This was in keeping with the experimental ethos of the new degree and it reflected a wider culture of playfulness and creativity that I detected was becoming more mainstream in the digital era of knowledge production and dissemination. For some, this issue of trying things out 'in public' may be at odds with the sometimes secretive world of research. There are issues of 'priority' and a PhD is supposed to 'add to human knowledge', which can be difficult if you give your ideas away early. If these issues are a concern to you, you can still use blogging to develop your more experimental ideas, or even to blog about the very secretiveness and closedness of academic research and the problems therewith!

This early feeling of playfulness and experimentation that I embraced is something I think is still important to keep in mind when blogging – even with academic blogging:

> *Generally your readers, whoever they are, will be more generous about creative and experimental work on blogs because such knowledge production*

does not come with the baggage of expectations associated with peer-reviewed articles and more traditional methods of publication.

So I was ready to go, but how to get started?

Technicalities and starting out

Although I had worked closely and in detail with a web designer on the architecture of the Arts and Sciences website and done a little basic coding and web writing myself (e.g. on Wikipedia pages), I did not set up my personal blog myself. In 2011, I was fortunate enough to be working on a charity website project with Jayson Winters from Brace Design. Jayson was himself learning about websites and blogsites at that time and kindly agreed to help me set up my own as part of the learning process. We experimented with layouts, structures, and so on, but Jayson handled the technical parts of the set-up. If, at this point, you are disappointed that I will not address the more technical 'backend' of blogging and are therefore considering whether to read on: stay! First, things have moved on a lot since 2011 and sites like Weebly have greatly simplified the set-up process. Second, the point of blogging is not the technical aspects but everything that comes after.

> *In short: you can certainly start a blog yourself on any one of several do-it-yourself sites or you could work with someone who would be interested in collaborating with you to set up the basics.*

Blogging was, in a stark sense, the only realistic outlet for my academic thinking in 2011. I was then far from the relevant knowledge networks that might help me progress in my thinking and I was unknown to most practitioners who might help me with the practicalities of developing a degree programme. Furthermore, I was not familiar with the culture of the relevant academic journals, as I had not followed the typical PhD, post-doc track. In a way that is hard to overemphasize, blogging helped me 'come in from the outside' to connect with the wider network, first, as a distant and somewhat detached node, but gradually as someone more central, involved in their own, meaningful and productive networks. Joining Twitter at the same time, in August 2011, was also key in building my network. I guess I would be categorized, therefore, as a fairly late adopter of blogging and an early- to mid-adopter of Twitter – at least for academic purposes.

> *It is never too early or too late to start blogging. However and whenever you do it, blogging will help you clarify your own ideas and form helpful networks.*

As an example of this, my friend and mentor – the eminent mathematical geographer Sir Alan Wilson – told me recently that he used my blogs as inspiration to start his own, after decades of writing books and doing formal academic research (Wilson, 2017). When discussing this chapter with Alan, he told me that he is now using his blogs as the basis for chapters in his new book – another example of how blogs can feed directly into conventional academic work.

Early blogs

The Arts and Sciences BASc has a remit to cover literally every discipline taught at UCL. In 2011, I had a decent knowledge of a wide range of disciplines, but I was relatively weaker in economics. As economics is currently very popular with students and dominates a lot of our daily discourse, I took some time to educate myself in economics and to blog about what I was learning (Gombrich, 2011). No doubt much of this writing was quite naïve. But such an approach doesn't matter so long as you make clear the purpose of the blog and provide sufficient caveats to alert your readers – something you couldn't do in more formal writing.

> *Again, much as with being creative, you can make mistakes in a blog and correct and retract things later; it is less likely these will be held as a black mark against you, so long as you are open and transparent about the process, include proper citations and references when due, and so on.*

In many of my early blogs, I stressed the value of conversation and dialogue in learning and did my best to keep the tone as informal as possible, while still being serious. As an example of this, I experimented with the idea of Academic vlogging (Gombrich, 2012). I made short videos on academic subjects and spoke about 'academic performance' through the ages and how this might change in the digital age of immediate transmission. Although, in the end, these ideas were not widely picked up, they did lead to interesting and affirming relationships with colleagues at other universities and were part of the pleasure of experimenting and playing (Lingard, 2013).

I didn't tweet out to a wider public many of these early blogs, as I knew they were experimental and possibly naïve. However, as I read and wrote more on interdisciplinarity, liberal arts and sciences, and – what became particular interests of mine – the ideas of generalism, polymathy, and the knowledge economy and its connection to contemporary higher education, I started to feel more confident about disseminating my work and began to tweet it out in order to publicize it, gain feedback, and build a network.

But the first topic that connected blogging, new networks, and my nascent academic career was a new trend in e-learning.

Taking off

My early blogs on 'flipping' lectures gave me the first experience of building knowledge networks related to a particular subject, and a glimpse of how personal blogging on academic subjects could have widespread positive ramifications.

Once again, I was by no means an instigator in this area. Indeed, subsequently Steve Wheeler remarked to me (and was surely justified in doing so) that such 'flipping' techniques had been around for years, so were hardly worth commenting on (Wheeler, 2012). However, for me the engagement became significant, especially when I presented some work on flipping lectures for a Higher Education Academy (HEA) workshop at UCL in Spring 2012. In academia, I could be thought of as an early adopter of 'flipping' – and I still remain an advocate, although, naturally perhaps, these days there is a more considered view of the pros and cons. In any event, I think my session for the HEA was popular because I was clearly not a technical wizard. The presentation probably went down well because it was not intimidating to any techno-resistant academics. This workshop and the blogs that preceded and followed it led to my presenting online webinars and further HEA workshops around the UK, and my blog was shared on the websites of other universities. Although such things may not seem so remarkable now, there is an element of hindsight in this more dismissive view. At the time there was in fact an explosion of interest around MOOCs and various other aspects of digital learning which Web 2.0 was beginning to make accessible to non-expert users for the first time. My early forays were both inspired by and played into this early excitement.

Blogging and tweeting can lead quickly to surprising uptakes and invitations: be prepared to engage with these! In my experience, the learning that comes from these invitations is invariably positive.

Although I have moved a little away from this area of interest now, the blogs on flipping lectures and the extra-institutional links to my work in this area remain important items of record and something I feature as part of my CV for internal promotions.

What makes an 'academic' blog?

There is a simple answer to this question: a blog written by an academic! More seriously, I don't think you should fret too much over whether your blog is 'academic' enough or not. New media challenge many of our ideas about writing, researching and referencing – and this is as it should be. A better definition of an academic blog might be one that attempts to address an intellectual issue seriously, citing sources and evidence where appropriate. Generally, these will be written by academics, although again, just what we mean by an 'academic' is coming under strong challenge and we should be aware that a great deal of interesting thought and research can come from people outside formal institutions of learning (Gombrich, 2013).

More important than whether a blog is sufficiently 'academic' or not is a desire and ability to engage with a wider audience as peers. In an immediate sense, your 'peers' for academic blogging are people with internet access,

rather than a small group of individuals schooled in a similar way to yourself.
This means you should be prepared to engage with any and all comments or
interactions in a friendly but direct, non-technical way.

Creating or dumping? Purpose and style of a blog

I am fairly relaxed about what I put on my blog in terms of format or style. Some
of what I think are my most important pieces – those that I have referenced in
more formal work (see below) – are created and written specially for the blog.
For these pieces I tend to use hyperlinks as references, as this seems more natural
in a piece written specially for the web.

However, I have also dumped some academic pieces I have given elsewhere
directly onto the blog. These are pieces that may not be of the right format for
journal publication but which I would still like to share with a wider audience.
For these pieces I tend to use standard academic referencing, as they were prepared
this way for a conference or other presentation.

These latter pieces are generally less read and I will tend to tweet them out
less, as I am conscious that the style may not be best suited for a blog. However,
they are often an integral part of my thinking and so it feels appropriate to have
them on the blog. (It also means that I have an easy way to find and refer to my
own work for future citations.)

Some blogs are long and some are very short.

With personal blogs, a wide range of styles and lengths of work is acceptable,
so long as you make clear to your readers what you are doing and what your
intentions with the blog are.

I admire the blogs of Steve Wheeler, Donald Clark (who has a penchant for
numbered lists), Greg Ashman, Tom Bennett, and others, and they are certainly
more consistent in their style and length than I am, but the eclectic approach
works for me and my blog can serve multiple purposes, as outlined here (Ashman,
2017; Bennett, 2017; Clark, 2017; Wheeler, 2017).

Building the networks

My blog readership is smallish. My most read blogs have around 2,000 hits each.
But it is not the absolute readership numbers that have been significant for me,
rather the networks that blogging and tweeting have allowed me to form and
which have had significantly benefited my career. For the purpose of brevity,
I will discuss in a little detail just two of the more important networks most closely
connected to blogging and then briefly summarize the rest. These two important
networks relate to: (1) generalism and polymathy, and (2) intra-institutional
relationships.

Generalism and polymathy network

Through some relatively early blogs on generalism and polymathy, inspired by the work of Peter Burke, and through tweeting out such blogs, I came into contact with Richard Martin (Burke, 2010; Mikkelsen and Martin, 2016). We discovered a shared interest in trying to make sense of a complex of ideas around education, personality traits, interests, skills, knowledge, and work that coalesces around the idea of *generalism* (as opposed to 'specialism'). 'Specialism' has become almost synonymous with 'expert', or even 'excellence', over the past 200 years or so, but specialists were not always so desirable and Richard and I are interested to reclaim the idea of generalism as a positive outcome for education and as a concept necessary for success in many contemporary white-collar jobs. This is not an area in which many academics are working and so meeting Richard and then his colleague Kenneth Mikkelsen, as well as the poet and explorer Robert Twigger (who writes on polymathy) – all through new media networks, rather than more usual academic channels – has been important in helping me build contemporary conceptualizations of generalism and polymathy, and in enriching my academic work.

Blogging and tweeting – especially using hashtags on key themes, e.g. (in my case) #generalism, #polymathy – can help you find collaborators and build academic networks in surprising places. Such collaborators in networks outside academia can certainly help your academic career. As one further example of this, in 2016 I was approached by The Economist to lead an event on the 'Future of Work' (hashtag #FoW) at UCL, which is already leading to further possible academic work.

Intra-institutional networks

Within my institution, UCL, there are of course many bloggers and tweeters. Blogging has helped me connect across the institution with those involved in this world. However, it has also helped me connect with management and service sectors within the organization that would have been almost inconceivable before the advent of social media and Web 2.0. It is difficult to quantify exactly what this means but I am sure that it has raised my profile within the institution in a positive way and given me a voice and a connection with people that I would otherwise not have had.

If you are employed by an academic institution, blogging and tweeting will almost certainly help you join up with parts of your institution that you might otherwise not be in contact with. This generally leads to greater collegiality and an understanding of shared mission.

Other networks

For some of the networks in which I am involved, it is difficult to distinguish whether they have formed mainly as a result of blogging or tweeting, or a combination of both.

But just to mention a few of them: I value my network of people involved in the world of work, from theorists like Richard Martin and Kenneth Mikkelsen, to HR professionals like Mervyn Dinnen or entrepreneurs like Sunil Malhotra from whom I learn about desirable attributes of graduates or employment assessment procedures. These thinkers have certainly engaged with at least one of my blogs and this has led to productive dialogues and meetings. Then, of course, there are countless thinkers in the education and e-education space from whom I have learned about connectivism, enforced independence, being a digital scholar, and other important concepts that are forming around learning and scholarship in the digital age (see, for example, Downes, 2012; Cormier, 2014). And, finally, there are networks of scholars (both early career and more established) with whom I share my blogs about interdisciplinarity.

> *Of course, these connections do not happen entirely automatically: a certain amount of searching and communicating is required. Although it may be more in keeping with my nature to do this and come more easily for someone interested in interdisciplinarity and generalism, in fact even the most isolated specialist will benefit from 'near-discipline' contacts and exchanges of ideas. By exploring even at the fringes of a specialism, you are likely to find ideas that will complement your own. Blogging and tweeting will facilitate finding these ideas.*

Relationship to traditional academic work

The relationships I have built through blogging and tweeting have led directly to more formal academic work, and this I find one of the most important developments to highlight – especially to more traditionally minded academics who may be sceptical of digital trends. Furthermore, through Twitter, and reading *his* blogs, I have found a collaborator in Michael Hogan with whom I have now written one chapter (for the *Oxford Handbook of Interdisciplinarity*, 2016) and am working on another paper.

Alongside the fact that blogging and tweeting networks have thus led directly to the production of more traditional academic work, there are also interesting shifts in what are regarded as acceptable sources and citations for more traditional writing. For example, in chapters in the second edition of the *Oxford Handbook of Interdisciplinarity* (Gombrich and Hogan, 2016) and in the recent Palgrave Macmillan book on *Experiences in Liberal Arts and Science Education from America, Europe, and Asia* (Gombrich, 2016), I reference my personal blog more than once as evidence and background to my thinking. These references have never been queried by the editors, although it is clear that the blog posts have not been through the usual peer review procedure of standard academic work. You could argue that as the editors have accepted me as an authority to write on the subject, they will naturally accept my blogs as sources as well. Nevertheless, citing material that is not peer-reviewed in an academic context represents a shift in convention.

Strategy and time investment

The simple flow chart shown in Figure 4.1 summarizes the preceding paragraphs and shows how my blogging has led to multiple productive outcomes.

> *If I can be said to have a strategy to blogging, the flow chart encapsulates it. Unquestionably, for my career blogging has been worth the time investment.*

Challenges and recognition

In my experience, formal recognition for blogging and tweeting are slow in coming. There are attempts to help academics create impact with social media but the way this works is usually by using blogging and social media to promote more traditional publications, rather than helping to promote the social media

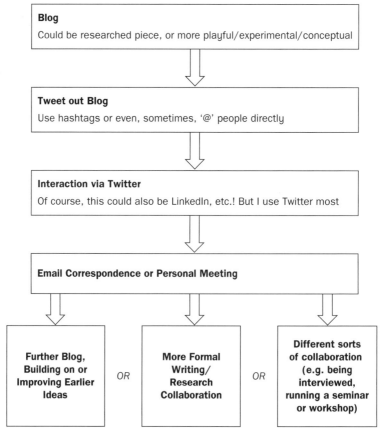

Figure 4.1   Flowchart to illustrate the process of planning and writing blogs

work itself. Thus, despite much talk of the importance of impact, outreach, engagement, and so on, the formal academic routes to promotion are struggling to recognize academic blogging and tweeting.

This may be changing slightly, however. I am currently working on an application for a fellowship of the Higher Education Academy and my institution has encouraged me to include information and data about my blogging where appropriate.

Although there are undoubtedly still barriers to having blogs accepted as 'proper' academic work, you can, through the methods discussed above, still make the blogs a vital adjunct to more traditional work. And there are some signs that more formal recognition of blogging and tweeting may be coming.

Two ironies and an unknown

I cannot conclude these reflections on academic blogging without noting two ironies and an unknown. Even in an age of opportunity for more informal academic writing, we must never lose touch with the critical approach and more sceptical stance appropriate to the academic mission! First, the ironies.

One of the ironies is benign; the other maybe less so. The benign irony is about being asked to contribute to a book called *The Digitally Agile Researcher* – because I am anything but digitally agile. As an example, I tried several times during this writing process to record a video piece for the Digitally Agile blog, but in the end gave up because I couldn't format the file to the right size and shape. I trust this is a benign irony, however, because it shows that you really don't have to be 'technically' inclined at all to get a great deal out of blogging. Once you stumble and clunk through the technical bit (as I have done several times, such as with my work on academic vlogging or with flipping lectures), the joy and benefits come from the networks formed, communications received, and other learning experiences and career advances that open up to you following interaction and dissemination via social media.

The less benign irony is that as I have become more established as an academic over the last two or three years, I have blogged less and less. The reasons for this are very simple: I am now using my 'writing time' to write more formal pieces for more formal publications. This is unfortunate. But if I want to further my career and, indeed, continue to build the evidential and intellectual base for the BASc in particular and interdisciplinary education in general, it is imperative that I write more 'peer-reviewed' work in more standard journals and books. That is how the system currently works and you can only buck the system for so long without ending up outside it and irrelevant to it. Until there are clear criteria for assessing the value of new forms of academic publishing, it seems inevitable that this will be the case. Although John Stepper's idea of 'working out loud' is valuable and might encourage academic bloggers to keep blogging while they are drafting more formal papers, the practicalities of this are not straightforward and the default pull, back to the private desktop and the personal word document, is strong (Stepper, 2015). I sincerely hope this situation changes in the near future and more widely accepted ways to credit academics with blogging and other social media work emerge, but we are not there yet.

So much for the 'ironies'. The 'unknown' arises thus: although I am immensely positive about blogging and, indeed, in some ways it has been the making of me as a thinker in my particular conceptual space of interdisciplinary education, what I cannot know is how much my position – as a relatively senior employee at a world-leading university like UCL – encouraged others to take my blogs more seriously than they might have done had I been a more junior person at a less well-known institution.

My intuition, though, is that 'quality will out'. Indeed, in my discussion with Alan Wilson, mentioned above, he too confirmed that high-quality work always becomes known eventually, whatever format or medium it is delivered in. No matter who you are or where you work, if you write well enough, have something of interest to say to others, and are brave yet courteous in connecting with them, your networks will form organically and your blogging will help you progress in many ways, several of which you could not have foreseen.

Concluding thoughts and the way ahead

I have a dilemma. A couple of years ago, I collected some interesting and suggestive data on the correlation between academic interests and leadership roles taken up by students at schools. I've wanted to publish a paper based on this data for some time. Should I go down the formal journal route or publish directly on my blog? The formal route will require much more work. First, I will need to read widely in areas (especially leadership studies) with which I am not familiar. Second, I will need to scope out the right journals. Third, the paper will need to be of a certain style and certain length to be acceptable. All this will add up to a delay in publication.

Some of these constraints are good constraints. They will require me to be rigorous and to do a lot of background reading, which should help me avoid taking false turns, repeating work that has been done before or making errors. And, of course, if the paper is published, it will be good for my traditional CV and academic status. But, supposing I do all this and get the paper published in 6–12 months' time. How many people will read it? What kind of impact will it make and what meaningful dialogue will it spark?

If, on the other hand, I publish this paper – written more freely, though still carefully and properly referenced – on my blog, I'm pretty sure I could get hundreds of readers, if not thousands. 'Leadership' is an easy hashtag with which to garner clicks and the nexus of 'education' and 'leadership' that the paper taps into would lead quickly to large networks of interest. This, therefore, is the dilemma:

> *Conventional paper: more peer review; possibly more rigour; tedious time delays and 'academic game-playing' with regard to style, jargon, journal, etc.; probably less readership, better for CV.*
>
> *VS*
>
> *Blog: probably wider readership; more interaction; probably more impact in terms of reaching people and gaining further opportunities; greater possibility of error; less highly regarded for CV; more timely publication.*
>
> *What do you think I should do?*

Finally, as I am completing this chapter on 11 July 2016, I take a moment out to check my LinkedIn pages. There I read this from Russell Schwartz, a US-based learning consultant:

> In my practice, I do a lot of informal research. My methodology is a lot like Action Research. Often I summarize my findings and recommendations in a paper. The quality of my work is probably not high enough to be published in a journal, and I will probably never be invited to present at a conference. But I believe my methods are fairly sound and that the papers contain value-adding information.

The author then gives an interesting 'sample abstract' about the effect of the civil war in Liberia on the curriculum there and he ends his LinkedIn comment, 'Do you have any interest in seeing these kinds of informal papers?'

I replied to this post to ask Russell why he needed to go down a 'formal' route and why he couldn't just start a blog and then begin to form networks of people interested in his material. He replied that he had just been on an online marketing course that had advised him to do exactly this! This example shows, I think, that the issue of blogging for academic purposes is alive and relevant. Furthermore, the related issue of what constitutes 'academic' work and what does not is one we will certainly be discussing in the years to come.

References

Ashman, G. (2017) *Filling the pail* [retrieved from: http://gregashman.wordpress.com].

Bennett, T. (2017) *Tom Bennett's School Report* [retrieved from: https://behaviourguru. blogspot.com].

Burke, P. (2010) The polymath: a cultural and social history of an intellectual species, in D.F. Smith and H. Philsooph (eds) *Explorations in Cultural History: Essays for Peter McCaffery* (pp. 67–79). Aberdeen: Centre for Cultural History.

Clark, D. (2017) *Donald Clark Plan B* [available at: http://donaldclarkplanb.blogspot.com].

Cormier, D. (2014) *Rhizomatic learning – The community is the curriculum* [retrieved from: https://courses.p2pu.org/en/courses/882/content/1797/].

Downes, S. (2012) *Connectivism and connective knowledge* [retrieved from: http://www.downes.ca/post/58207].

Gombrich, C. (2011) *Carl Gombrich: Education, interdisciplinarity, expertise – economics* [retrieved from: http://www.carlgombrich.org/category/economics/page/3/].

Gombrich, C. (2012) *Carl Gombrich: Education, interdisciplinarity, expertise – academic vlogging II* [retrieved from: http://www.carlgombrich.org/academic-vlogging-ii/].

Gombrich, C. (2013) *Carl Gombrich: Education, interdisciplinarity, expertise – the new amateurism* [retrieved from: http://www.carlgombrich.org/the-new-amateurism/].

Gombrich, C. (2016) Polymathy, new generalism and the future of work: a little theory and some practice from UCL's Arts and Sciences degree, in W. Kirby and M. van der Wende (eds) *Experiences in Liberal Arts and Science Education from America, Europe and Asia: A dialogue across continents* (pp. 75–89). London: Palgrave Macmillan.

Gombrich, C. and Hogan, M.J. (2016) Interdisciplinarity and the student voice, in R. Frodeman, J.T. Klein and R.C.S. Pacheo (eds) *The Oxford Handbook of Interdisciplinarity*, 2nd edn. (pp. 544–557). Oxford: Oxford University Press.

Lingard, M. (2013) *Reluctant technologist: my first video blog post* [retrieved from: https://mattlingard.wordpress.com/2013/01/04/my-first-video-blog-post/].

London School of Economics (LSE) (2017) *LSE Impact Blog* [retrieved from: http://blogs.lse.ac.uk/impactofsocialsciences/tag/academic-blogging/].

Mikkelsen, K. and Martin, R. (2016) *The Neo-Generalist: Where you go is who you are.* London: LID Publishing.

Snow, C.P. (1993) *The Two Cultures*. Cambridge: Cambridge University Press.

Stepper, J. (2015) *Working Out Loud*. New York: Ikigai Press.

Wheeler, S. (2012) *Learning with 'e's: what the flip?* [retrieved from: http://www.steve-wheeler.co.uk/2012/03/what-flip.html].

Wheeler, S. (2017) *Learning with 'e's* [retrieved from: http://www.steve-wheeler.co.uk/].

Wilson, A. (2017) *Quaestio: Research: questioning, inquiring, seeking, searching and scruitinising* [retrieved from: http://quaestio.blogweb.casa.ucl.ac.uk/].

5

The Conversation: writing for the general public and how to keep on top of new research

Gemma Ware and Michael Parker

Introduction

The twenty-first century is so far proving a difficult time for the business of producing news. As more and more readers swap print for digital, advertising revenue is declining, putting pressure on newsrooms to produce more content with ever-fewer resources. Social media has radically changed the way people find and receive information: many readers allow the content to come to them rather than heading to news providers' websites where their presence can be monetized through advertising. As editor of *The Guardian* Kath Viner has argued, with the expectation of cost-free content and services that the internet has brought, news organizations face tough questions as to how, and how much, to charge consumers for quality content – or indeed whether they're willing to pay at all (Viner, 2016).

At the same time, recent structural changes in the way that research is judged in the UK through the Research Excellence Framework (REF) and its associated impact agenda mean that now more than ever researchers are encouraged by universities to communicate the findings of their research to the wider public.

These two trends have opened up a role for academics to communicate their own research, and also to use their expertise to explain new or complex issues to the general public. One platform set up specifically to bring academic expertise to a broader audience by publishing articles written by academics is The Conversation, where the two of us are editors.

In this chapter, we first explain the rationale behind The Conversation and the benefits for contributing academics, as well as giving some tips for researchers who want to write for the general public. We then explain the channels that journalists use to keep on top of new research and developments, before listing some tools that could be useful for academics to keep abreast of new research in their field.

Public engagement and The Conversation

The Conversation is a news website like any other in that it carries articles on people, places, and events in the news, comment and opinion on current affairs, and new research. Where it differs from other publications is that it is entirely written by academics and researchers, drawn from institutions all over the world. The Conversation's team of professional journalists seek out and commission articles from academics with the right expertise to provide insight and analysis to the topic in hand, and then apply their editorial skills to ensure the final article will appeal to a broad, non-academic audience.

Generating dozens of articles a week, the result feels somewhere between a general interest newspaper and a special interest magazine: the big events of the day are covered, but so are little-discussed but interesting or important issues, and new developments from the world of research. Everything is presented in such a way that the articles may be understood by a general reader, rather than requiring, or assuming, any specialist knowledge of the subject.

The arrival of the REF agenda in the UK and its emphasis on impact and public dissemination of research was not a factor behind the creation of The Conversation, but the two dovetail neatly together: universities and academics see their work and expertise spread widely, the general public – who through taxation fund universities in the first place – get to learn from the fruits of academia's labour, and the quality of public debate and ultimately policy-making is raised through the application of facts and expertise.

Bringing back the experts

The defining characteristic of the media landscape in the first 15 years of the twenty-first century century has been the impact of the internet on news businesses. As audiences move from print to internet-based media, newspaper and magazine readership figures drop, and advertising and classified advertising moves online where rates are low. This has caused newsrooms and journalism to suffer.

This is one of the factors that led to the creation of The Conversation, the brainchild of British journalist Andrew Jaspan – former editor of *The Scotsman*, the *Sunday Herald*, and *The Observer* in the UK, and *The Age* in Melbourne – and Jack Rejtman, an American business strategy consultant working in Australian higher education. Explaining the circumstances that led to founding of The Conversation in a TEDx talk in 2012, Jaspan said:

> Globally, newspapers are in real trouble. Many are being shut, others merged, journalists are being laid off. And because of that, the quality of journalism has declined and trust in journalism has waned. Newsrooms have been hollowed out, particularly specialists. By those I mean environment, science, health and other specialist reporters – usually the most expensive journalists – have been taken out and replaced with cheaper, generalist journalists, generally younger and less experienced, and this gives only a shallower offering back to the public.

With a loss of specialist reporters, in-depth understanding of topics has given way to more superficial treatments that fail to sufficiently air and analyse the underlying causes of and solutions to the issues of the day.

At the same time, the enormous amount of information online has led to reporting-by-Google-search – yet the internet's signal-to-noise ratio can be very low indeed, and misinformation and error abound. This lack of in-depth understanding of subjects, with fewer editorial staff required to produce ever more content, has led to what has been called 'churnalism' (Davies, 2008a). In *Flat Earth News*, journalist Nick Davies' broadside against the malaise afflicting the media describes in unflinching detail how through lack of expertise and time and business pressures, press releases, PR-inspired stories, and outright fabrications become commonplace in newspapers (Davies, 2008b).

But readers for the most part are not fooled, and are well aware of the declining quality of content; when that translates into fewer sales, this only adds to newspapers' problems. The answer, Jaspan explained in his TEDx talk (2012), was to turn once more to experts:

> It occurred to me that a university is not unlike a newsroom: you have your faculties of business, science, arts, and within them you have politics departments and so on. But within those departments were real specialists, truly smart people who had spent their entire career studying a subject, not just at that university but within their peer networks internationally. If you have to write about a tsunami, you will be able to tap into everybody you know who studies the Earth's crust throughout the world – that's the knowledge network that academics bring.

Universities are knowledge creators, while newspapers are knowledge disseminators. The trick was to bring them together, inspiration for which came from a conversation with Nobel Laureate virologist Doherty. Jaspan (2012) recalls:

> Instead of sitting across the table from me as a journalist, he said, I'd like you to sit next to me. I'd like you to help me write in a way that is readable and engaging, but which allows me to honor the integrity of the science and the facts that I have.

Following several years of development and with encouragement from Glyn Davis, vice-chancellor of the University of Melbourne, The Conversation launched in March 2011 (Quinn, 2011) with a team of 12 editors and funding from universities, the Australian federal government and the state of Victoria, and the Commonwealth Bank of Australia.

A not-for-profit charitable trust, The Conversation is essentially a membership organization funded chiefly by contributing universities. The universities provide funding, academic authors provide their time and expertise, and both benefit from The Conversation's editors' journalistic skills and the publishing platform that carries the content to readers far and wide.

The same model has since been replicated in other countries. A UK bureau (TCUK) was established at City, University of London and launched in May 2013, with 13 supporting universities and seven editors. This has since expanded to 75 universities and 25 editors. A US bureau (TCUS) initially based at Boston University launched in October 2014, whose team has expanded to include offices in New York and Atlanta. A third bureau in Africa (TCAfrica), based in Johannesburg, South Africa, launched in 2015 and has expanded with an office in Nairobi, Kenya. Later that year the first non-English language edition launched, with a French language edition established in Paris, France (TCF). July 2017 saw the launch of our sixth regional edition, TC Canada, based in Toronto and Vancouver.

This geographic spread creates what we call a 'virtual global newsroom', capable of providing coverage around the world and around the clock. Relevant content is shared between the regional bureaus, and all articles are published at theconversation.com, with the reader able to switch between regional editions. The Conversation's editorial guidelines are governed by a charter, and each bureau is governed by an editorial board that includes both senior members of academia and the media (The Conversation, 2017a).

It has been eight years since *Flat Earth News* was published, yet only this summer Michael Gove, a former Secretary of State for Education for the UK government no less, declared on Sky News during the EU referendum campaign that 'we have had enough of experts' (Mance, 2016). In a world in which facts are hard to pin down while expertise too often remains cloistered and inaccessible, The Conversation's aim is to provide the means to bring expertise and understanding to the public sphere where it is needed.

Partnering with academia – a business model

A key element in The Conversation's approach of spreading knowledge, rather than adopting a 'walled-garden' business model common among academic publications, is that all content is published under an open access licence (The Conversation, 2017b). This Creative Commons licence (CC-BY-ND) means that all content is free to read and free for others to republish – without alteration, and with original credit to the author, institution and The Conversation as original publisher intact (Creative Commons, 2017).

Through republication in other outlets, authors writing for The Conversation are able to access the much larger readerships of other established publications, from major newspapers, magazines, and online publishers to much smaller internet-only websites. In October 2016, 3.8 million unique users visited the site from around the world, with a readership of 27 million including republication.

This model meets two needs: for academia to do a better job of communicating its work and research, and for journalism to aid the public's understanding of complex topics through the expertise of those writing it.

Something many academics may be familiar with is how well, or not, academic writing is transposed into the media. Academics forged links with the media long before The Conversation arrived, and while many will have had the satisfaction of seeing their work written about and discussed, in some cases those talking to the media will have felt that their words or work were taken out of context or misrepresented. Leaving aside deliberate misrepresentation, the problem often lies in those occasions where turns of phrase, words or technical terms carry specific meanings for the writer and within their field of study, but not for the lay audience.

In an attempt to allay these concerns and encourage academics to write for The Conversation, academic authors must approve the final piece before publication. During the editorial process, editors will edit an article for clarity, sense, and length, which may introduce minor inaccuracies or change the language used. The real-time online content management system that powers theconversation.com and which is used by author and editor to create the article is designed so that the academic's sign-off is required, meaning that the author must first see and approve any changes or edits made to the piece before it is published.

Authors must fill out a disclosure statement, three straightforward questions regarding funding and affiliations that academics will not be unfamiliar with. One of the complaints of the mainstream media is of its opacity – who are the writers and owners, and where do their interests lie? By being up-front about funding and affiliations, readers can be assured that the only angle being pushed is that of learning about the subject in hand.

Finally, the site records and compiles detailed readership figures that are made available to authors and to member institutions. These records include readership figures, sites where articles have been republished and the readership the articles have received there, the article's mentions on social media, and global reach. Broken down into running totals and per-article statistics, these figures can be used by authors as part of, for example, funding bids to demonstrate readership, reach, and distribution of their research.

Not every academic is comfortable writing for the media or appearing in public. While The Conversation welcomes those that are, it is designed to encourage those that are not to take the plunge. Authors enjoy the editorial support of professional journalists, a safe writing and editing space, and pre-publication approval, while readers are brought a range of new and established expert voices in a wide range of topics. The REF means that academics are now under growing pressure to communicate their research and see that its findings and implications reach the public sphere. The Conversation, we would suggest, is the easiest, most editorially supportive way of doing that.

Writing for the public: tips and techniques

Writing on the subject of public engagement, Patrick Dunleavy, Professor of Political Science and Public Policy at the London School of Economics, is bold in his declaration of the importance of reaching beyond academic audiences (Dunleavy and Gilson, 2012). He states:

> A new research communications approach has grown up – one that de-emphasizes the traditional journals route, and re-prioritizes faster, real-time academic communication in which blogs play a critical intermediate role. They link to research reports and articles on the one hand, and they are linked to from

Twitter, Facebook and Google+ news-streams and communities. So in research terms blogging is quite simply, one of the most important things that an academic should be doing right now.

He offers good advice for academics, including six tips reworded for reproduction here. It is worth noting here that Dunleavy, among many others, emphasizes also the importance of using social media such as Twitter and Facebook in order to further disseminate your work but also to start conversations around it. Also on LSE blogs, World Bank economists David McKenzie and Berk Özler (2011) reveal how the use of social media, blogging, and other non-academic routes can have a direct and very apparent effect on the scale of the reach and impact of, for example, published journal articles and discussion of the topic. Use of social media is something that is discussed more fully by Steve Wheeler in Chapter 3 and Ian O'Byrne in Chapter 2 in this volume.

Patrick Dunleavy's public engagement tips for academics

- *Make sure your headlines tell the story, and make sure that the findings, conclusions, or point of each post are communicated early on.* Academics normally like to build up their arguments slowly, and then only tell you their findings with a final flourish at the end. And they often show great dedication in choosing obscure titles for their work. Don't do this 'Dance of the Seven Veils' in which layers of irrelevance are progressively stripped aside for the final kernel of value-added knowledge to be revealed. Instead, make sure that all the information readers need to understand what you're saying is upfront – you'll make a much stronger impression.
- *Don't leave readers wondering who's written the piece*: make sure your byline and biography are clear and accessible and up to date. This is also an opportunity to provide links to Twitter, LinkedIn, university profile, and so on. Profile photos are good too.
- *Newsy pieces of writing are timely, so be sure that the document is dated.* That way, readers can ascertain where the piece fits in the context of others on the subject. Of course, if it relates to something that's happened recently (a 'news hook'), then it goes without saying that should be up at the top.
- *The web is a network.* Use the various ways in which people come across content: social media like Facebook and Twitter, RSS, email newsletters, internal comms, departmental blogs, etc. And make use of hyperlinks to provide contextual references throughout the text to add value and provide in-depth material for those readers who want it. Don't use footnotes, don't cite every statement as if you would a journal article, but do provide evidence for claims – especially bold or controversial claims.
- *Wherever possible, lodge articles of lasting value in university depositories*, so they can be picked up by search crawlers or directories such as Google Scholar. This is important, and applies to peer-reviewed research as much as to general interest articles for public consumption. In general, only material that is lodged in open access repositories can be submitted to the REF, but

more importantly, research and writing that do not languish behind a paywall can be read and linked to by others.

- *Talk to your readers. Create conversations. Share.* Encourage people to comment, but moderate where necessary. Share your work and that of others. The aim is to improve the public understanding of complex, often important subjects. Do this well, and fame, fortune, and flourishing will follow naturally.

First steps

So, what makes a good story? Good starting points include:

- *An explanation of, comment on, or analysis of people, places, topics or events in the news.* 'In the news' can be quite broad. Sometimes an article can approach the subject of the news article that inspired it; in other cases, a single mention of another related topic within the original can be extracted and become the focus for a larger and more in-depth piece.
- *New or recent research* is always of interest, whether the author's own research or that of others in the author's field of expertise. Generally, writing about another's work is the better approach: our readers get two opinions for the price of one, and the piece comes across as less self-promoting. Try to give journalists as much forward notice of a paper's publication as possible.
- *Answer an interesting question.* Note 'interesting'. Posing rhetorical questions solely to launch into extremely technical or nuanced debates is discouraged. In general, articles should propose or be summed up as a statement – our readers come for answers, not questions.
- *Lists.* Like it or not, the Buzzfeedification of the news is well established. Lists ('Top 10 cities that . . . five ways you can get more out of . . . 27 dogs that just can't . . . ') are an easy and approachable way to provide a way into a subject for readers. For example, among The Conversation's most read articles are 'Five science "facts" we learnt at school that are plain wrong' and 'Five myths about the chemicals you breathe, eat and drink' by the University of Hull's Mark Lorch (2014a, 2014b).

Things to consider as stories include being:

- Dramatic
- New
- Explainers
- Unusual
- Questions
- Fun
- Lists
- Surprising
- Personal

- Universal
- Timeless
- Timely.

The key element is timeliness – prepare a response quickly so as to garner the interest of those following the story while it is current. Some topics come on and go off the boil within 24 hours, which means catching the story with one of your own before it is stale is a key element of working with the news cycle. On the other hand, some topics with longer lifespans are evergreen and so timeless, which can be published at any time.

You know you've got a good story if you can summarize it in one sentence. To do this you need to work out what your angle is by identifying the aspect of the story that would be most important or most interesting to your readers. Take a step back: what's interesting to the general public, rather than to a specialist with many years experience of the topic? It may not always be the aspect that is most important academically. And it's worth pointing out that this means you can't fit all your points into the piece. It's a case of isolating the most important, interesting, catchy or unusual and focusing on that while letting other aspects fall to the wayside.

The importance of the top-line test

An article with a strong angle is one that can be easily summed up in a catchy, pithy sentence that brings the article across in a way that makes readers want to read on. Here are two examples, from articles pitched to The Conversation, and how they were summed up in a headline – the 'top-line test' – by the editor:

1. I have interviews from Paris, Berlin and Barcelona where I interviewed digital activists in the last six months. There is a quieter digital activism of building platforms for civic purposes and cultural citizenship. Tech/artists involved in projects for digital inclusion against surveillance etc, which does not involve cyberattacks as with Anonymous or just using social media to mobilise protests, but builds community and is for public use as digital commons.

The top line: How a new wave of digital activists is changing society

2. Doomsday scenarios surrounding a robot apocalypse abound in popular science fiction, from *Battlestar Galactica* to *Terminator*. But working with machine intelligence in the lab is a methodical practice that can uncover innovative designs that can help humanity and enable us to learn how our own intelligence came about. My recent work has included designing a "mother" robot that can manufacture its own "children" without human intervention. In the process, it uses principles from nature, including natural selection, to produce incrementally superior generations that improve in performance on a specific task.

The top line: How we built a robot that can evolve – and why it won't take over the world

By working out the top line, it's easier to focus on what matters to tell the story and what is extraneous material that can be left out. This results in a more tightly written, focused piece that's more compelling and easier to read.

Writing style and tone

It's vital to think about the audience you're writing for: they are likely to be intelligent, educated, curious readers who are interested in learning more, but time is precious and attention spans are ever shortening. Readers are not prepared to wade through dense academic prose, and you should be prepared to change your style accordingly. Straight talking and use of the vernacular are not the same as 'dumbing down', and shouldn't be thought of as such. The purpose of communication is 'understanding'; if the reader cannot understand the language the writer uses, the effort of both reader and author is wasted. It's especially important to take heed of this point, when the house styles of so many academic journals tend to veer towards the impenetrable.

This example is a passage from a piece on how to tackle Ebola:

Before:

The current Ebola outbreak in West Africa has highlighted the challenges of implementing control actions in the face of severe scientific and public health uncertainties. A formalised approach to integrating the outcome of prediction models with clearly defined management objectives may help to facilitate an objective discussion of control actions and the information needed to most effectively implement control amid significant logistical constraints.

After:

The current Ebola outbreak in West Africa has highlighted the challenges of bringing in control measures in the face of severe scientific and public health uncertainties. By comparing proposed interventions we can highlight which are expected to save the most lives.

Compare the two versions. The question the writer should hold in their mind is: how much detail is necessary? While sometimes the detail *is* the story – a new technique to achieve something, or the details as reported by a witness to an event – more often the fine details can be safely dropped or summarized in the process of getting to the point.

Structure

The key structural element of journalistic writing is what is sometimes called the inverse news pyramid. This is really just a fancy way of saying 'get to the point'. All news writing is formed in this way, with a laser-like focus on the top line and commitment to communicating the point of the piece as quickly and clearly as possible.

For example, the first element of a piece is the headline. A headline should conjure up the essence of the article in a handful of words, in a way that persuades the reader to continue with the hundreds of words that follow. It is more an advert for the piece than an element of the piece itself.

Following the headline, the opening sentence and following sentences should get straight to the point, outlining the essence of the article's point or conclusions. Assume that you will lose 10 per cent of your readers with every sentence or paragraph. That way, if the reader left after the first paragraph, they would at least have the gist of what had occurred to prompt the article in the first place. They would know the piece's 'top line' (see box on p. 52). Further detail and analysis should be introduced progressively through the piece.

In essence, this means starting at the end: the conclusion, results, findings, recommendations – whatever encapsulates what you want readers to take away from the piece. Don't write chronologically, starting at the beginning and only getting to the end – and therefore the point – several paragraphs before the end of the piece, by which time many of your readers will have left.

Roy Peter Clark of the Poynter Institute, a journalism research centre in the US, has a list of 50 writing tools (Clark, 2006) that is an excellent source of stylistic and structural tips.

Writing for non-academic audiences should come to you naturally: it is, after all, how we communicate with each other outside our professional lives. With a bit of practice, writing for readers beyond those of your academic niche can be rewarding – and fun. Many Conversation authors speak of their fascination with the dashboard readership figures and the rapid turnaround that sees feedback arrive in hours and days, rather than months or years. Interest from other media frequently follows a published piece, and invitations to present papers at conferences, edit special editions of journals, get involved in academic collaborations, or present evidence to parliament are also common. Certainly, readers' appetite for the knowledge of experts is unabated. The Conversation's success is in connecting the two.

Common Pitfalls

- Jargon, especially 'managerese' and clichés.
- A shotgun approach to acronyms. Don't define an acronym if the word is not used again in the piece, and especially avoid TUA (totally unnecessary acronyms), where the author simply turns a set of words or phrase used frequently in a piece into an acronym.
- Over-formal or didactic tone. Fight against it, and avoid expressions like 'Of course . . . ', 'Naturally . . . ', 'Everybody knows that . . . '
- Falling into academic/essay style, such as a chronological approach or by writing in the introduction–method–results–conclusion style.
- Rhetorical questions.
- Headlines of the form: 'Initial statement: then a question?' Although headlines in the form of a question are sometimes a natural fit for a piece, readers invariably want answers, not to be faced with further questions. Turn questions into statements. After all, your piece is saying something – isn't it?
- Long sentences, excess use of (arguably, any use of) semi-colons.

Best Practice

- Get to the point, then fill in the detail.
- Don't assume readers' knowledge of the subject, but don't bury them in detail either.
- Short and punchy sentences.
- Properly explain any specialist terms that cannot be left out or worded around.
- Cut words ruthlessly.
- Use active not passive sentences.
- Be wary of too many '-ings': repeatedly using the participle adds weight to sentences and slows them down. Sentences with present, active verbs are clean, punchy, and easy to read.
- Reading your piece aloud is a great way to find weak spots.
- The first sentence/paragraph (known as the lead) and last (the payoff) are the hardest to write, but the most important. Often it's easier to write the piece and then go back to rewrite the intro based on how the piece turned out as you wrote it.
- Ideas needn't be simple; the language in which they are expressed should be.
- Don't be scared of humour.
- Consider Orwell's six rules, from 'Politics and the English Language' (Orwell, 1946).
- Make sure you answer these questions: Who? What? Why? Where? When? How?
- Feel free to have an opinion, but back it up with facts and research.

How journalists find out about research, and what you can learn from them

In this section, we explain how journalists keep on top of new research and offer some tools for academics to do so too. Most journalists find out about academic research because it is press released – by a university, research council, funder, the journal that published it or because it had been presented at a large conference. In some fields, the dissemination of academic research to journalists is much more structured than in others.

For example, most science journalists will be signed up to a service called Eurekalert, which sends out daily email notifications with short summaries of embargoed press releases from a range of high-impact journals and directly from universities. Many journalists will also be signed up to receive weekly embargoed news alerts from specific journals such as *Science, Nature,* and the *Proceedings of the National Academy of Sciences.* These services are only available to journalists, but it's worth being aware if any paper you publish is going to make it onto one of these news alerts, as it will inevitably get more traction.

In the social sciences, these kinds of curated lists of embargoed press releases are rarer, and journalists are more likely to become aware of upcoming research by a press release directly from a university, a research council such as the ESRC or AHRC, or by being on the press release list of a think tank, civil society group or charity that has worked with the academic. This means that individual relationships with academics, tips about new projects, and who is working on what area are very valuable to individual journalists.

First steps: keeping abreast of research

As an academic, you should play to your advantages. Unlike most journalists, who probably know a handful of academics in the fields or sector that they cover and keep coming back to them, you can develop a network around the world in your field. This network can give you a valuable insight into new projects and publications.

As detailed in Chapter 3 on social media engagement, Twitter has become a key tool for researchers for a number of reasons. By following the feeds of key journals and other academics in your field, Twitter can become a key source to find out about new journal releases. Hashtags can be a good way of finding older tweets, for example, that are linked to a particular conference or event, or related to a particular piece of statistical software or method. For instance, the hashtag #qgis is used by those who use the QGIS open source map creation software. However, Twitter can also be a fairly blunt instrument because of the magnitude of information in a stream. In order not to miss out hearing about other research in your field, there are some other useful tools.

Academic research networks

You may find it useful to sign up to use an academic social network, such as academia.edu (see also Chapter 7), to help you with your research curation. It is possible to identify key papers that are relevant to your research as you are writing, which are then made public. Dr. Jana Javornik, senior lecturer in public and social policy at the University of East London, said about academia.edu:

> [It] has this editorial system in place where you as the user kind of identify key papers that are relevant to your work and then you make it public to your followers . . . this is what I want to bookmark, this is what I want to read, this is what I am reading, which also helps me because I get alerts of what people that matter to my work are reading and what they are engaging with and I can quickly identify whether this is relevant to my work or not and I can follow up . . . It's like doing free work. As you are looking for research that is relevant to your work, you are helping to create lists for your colleagues as well.

Scholarly email lists

A good way to keep up to date with new projects and research is through scholarly email lists. Run by JISCM@il, these are large lists linked to a field or issue, for example, urban geography or European social policy. If you prefer not to receive a huge volume of traffic, it's possible not to get the email alerts, but to bookmark the list serve in your browser to check back when you want to. New content and good and valuable posts rise to the top because people have reacted to them, acting as a sort of filter.

Journal alerts and RSS feeds

To make sure you never miss any papers published by the key journals in your field, you could sign up to email alerts via the publishers themselves. An alternative, if you prefer using an RSS feed reader such as Feedly.com or Netvibes, is to subscribe to RSS feeds from particular journals or new posts from academic blogs. The volume can be large, so it is important to be selective: prioritize quality not quantity.

Google Scholar alerts

It is possible to sign up for alerts via the Google Scholar platform to receive email notifications when particular academics or researchers publish a paper, or when they are cited in a paper. This can also be a good way of monitoring citations of your own work (through the Google Scholar Citations part of the platform), as well as those in your department or academics around the world whose research is close to or relevant to your own.

Parliamentary alerts

This is a service that will be most useful to academics researching areas that are impacted by government policy. With a plethora of Bills and select committees in the process when the House of Commons and House of Lords are in session, a good way to keep abreast of what is being discussed is to receive alerts. At www.parliament.uk you can subscribe for alerts when certain select committees, such as the Public Account Select Committee or the Education Select Committee, are sitting. This can be particularly useful to find out which stakeholders (including academics) will be giving evidence to a committee.

You can also follow the progress of particular Bills, such as the Higher Education and Research Bill, by clicking to receive email alerts when the Bill is debated in one of the chambers, or a vote is scheduled.

For those interested in following the activity of a particular MP, it's also possible to sign up via the website www.theyworkforyou.com to get email notifications whenever a particular MP or Lord speaks or asks a written question.

Building a relationship with journalists

It is important to remember that journalists, working in increasingly smaller newsrooms with squeezed budgets, are under a lot of pressure and faced with tight deadlines. As a result, they can be quite demanding when they need to ask you questions about a new paper that they want to cover, but sometimes difficult to get hold of when you have an event or a piece of research that you would like covered.

As mentioned above, many press releases are sent out on a mass scale to a wide range of journalists. Once a piece of research has been press released, it has a certain lifespan. This is because newspapers often do not like to be seen to be late to the party: if their rival published an article about a piece of research on Tuesday, it's unlikely they would do so the following day. Of course, there are exceptions to this, particularly for longer feature articles or more in-depth radio segments, or where journalists are looking to get academic opinion to help them explain a bit of legislation going through parliament.

While frustrating, this constraint can provide opportunities to create mutually beneficial relationships with journalists that you trust. They will be looking for research that has not been widely press released elsewhere so that they can get a 'scoop'. The press team at your university should be a good point of contact to find out which journalists might be a good fit for you, and whether it would be worth offering them a piece of research as an 'exclusive'. If a journalist has spoken to you before or knows you have researched or are researching a particular issue, and the interaction went well, they will be more likely to come to you for comment again in future. If they feel comfortable ringing you up for background information about a complex issue or to explain a new research paper that they don't understand, they might be more willing to listen when you have something that you want to get their attention.

Something to remember: If you're comfortable working with a particular journalist and want to keep them within your network, make sure your mobile number is in your email signature. It can be frustrating for journalists on a tight deadline if they only have the office number of a researcher, or email address, but no way of reaching them immediately.

Timing is crucial

If you are trying to get your own research covered in a newspaper, or have a pitch taken by a platform like The Conversation, timing is crucial. Don't tell a journalist at 5.30 pm that your paper is coming out at midnight. Make sure you give them good warning. They might plan a longer feature, push for their article to make it onto the front page if this is ground-breaking research or highly relevant to an issue in the current news, or just simply need some time to create accurate graphs or maps to accompany the article.

If your area of research interest suddenly becomes headline news, do be ready and willing to write or speak about it for the general public. One example at The Conversation was when China announced it was finally ending its one child policy in October 2015. Stuart Gietel-Basten, Associate Professor of Social Policy at the University of Oxford, has studied demography and the impact on population policies in Asia for much of his career. When an editor at The Conversation emailed him to ask if he could write a quick reaction article to the news, he was sitting in an airport with a couple of hours to pass before a flight. He quickly wrote 700 words, approved the edits, and the article was published before he boarded (Gietel-Basten, 2015). When he landed many hours later, he had received a number of emails asking for comment from other journalists and his article had been read nearly 50,000 times. The timing was crucial.

Common Pitfalls

- As a young researcher, the noise of social media and possibilities offered by a more engaged approach to public communication can be very attractive. It is important to choose your interactions careful so as not to become overloaded. As James Borrell, a PhD student in biology at Queen Mary University London put it, while gaining experience in science communication as an early career researcher is 'really, really valuable', you mustn't do it 'at the expense of doing the science'. He said: 'I think a balance is really important.'
- It is possible to sign up for too many email alerts, so pick them carefully. If you get too many, you won't read them. It is up to you to choose a method of keeping abreast of new research in a manner that suits you and does not feel overwhelming. Perhaps that means taking an hour or so out of your week to look through alerts, certain Twitter hashtags or JISC list serves, rather than signing up to endless email alerts.

Best Practice

- Keep abreast of research and developments in your field by finding the best way of curating research that works for you. This will help you in your own research, but also provide opportunities to comment in public-facing fora such as The Conversation, blogs or other media, about new findings or developing policy in your area.
- Don't assume knowledge. When pitching an idea to a journalist, editor or even your university press officer, don't assume that they know what you're talking about. Imagine you were talking to a friend or family member who is not an academic. Be patient if they don't understand at first – this is your research and it will be of benefit to you if it can be presented in a way that is as accessible as possible to the general public.

Cited resources

Academia.edu [https://www.academia.edu]
Google Scholar [http://scholar.google.co.uk]
JiscMail [https://www.jiscmail.ac.uk/]
The Research Excellence Framework [www.ref.ac.uk]

They Work For You [https://www.theyworkforyou.com]
Twitter [http://twitter.com/LSEImpactBlog]
UK Parliament [www.parliament.uk]

References

Clark, R.P. (2006) Fifty writing tools: quick list, *Poynter: A global leader in journalism* [retrieved from: http://www.poynter.org/2006/fifty-writing-tools-quick-list/76067/].

Creative Commons (2017) *Attribution-NoDerivatives 4.0 International (CC-BY-ND 4.0)* [retrieved from: https://creativecommons.org/licenses/by-nd/4.0/].

Davies, N. (2008a) *Press Gazette*, 4 February [retrieved from: http://www.pressgazette. co.uk/nick-davies-churnalism-has-taken-the-place-of-what-we-should-be-doing-telling-the-truth-40117].

Davies, N. (2008b) *Flat Earth News: An award-winning reporter exposes falsehood, distortion and propaganda in the global media*. London: Chatto & Windus.

Dunleavy, P. and Gilson, Ch. (2012) Five minutes with Patrick Dunleavy and Chris Gilson: 'Blogging is quite simply, one of the most important things that an academic should be doing right now', *LSE blogs – The Impact Blog*, 24 February [retrieved from: http:// blogs.lse.ac.uk/impactofsocialsciences/2012/02/24/five-minutes-patrick-dunleavy-chris-gilson].

Gietel-Basten, S. (2015) Why scrapping the one-child policy will do little to change China's population, *The Conversation*, 29 October [retrieved from: https://theconversation.com/ why-scrapping-the-one-child-policy-will-do-little-to-change-chinas-population-49982].

Jaspan, A. (2012) A new way to do journalism: Andrew Jaspan at TEDxCanberra, *YouTube* [retrieved from: https://www.youtube.com/watch?v=SMGqpikuVEQ].

Lorch, M. (2014a) Five science 'facts' we learnt at school that are plain wrong, *The Conversation*, 28 October [retrieved from: https://theconversation.com/five-science-facts-we-learnt-at-school-that-are-plain-wrong-33258].

Lorch, M. (2014b) Five myths about the chemicals you breathe, eat and drink, *The Conversation*, 19 May [retrieved from: https://theconversation.com/five-myths-about-the-chemicals-you-breathe-eat-and-drink-26849].

Mance, H. (2016) We've had enough of experts, says Gove, *Financial Times*, 3 June [retrieved from: https://www.ft.com/content/3be49734-29cb-11e6-83e4-abc22d5d108c].

McKenzie, D. and Özler, B. (2011) Academic blogs are proven to increase dissemination of economic research and improve impact, *LSE blogs – The Impact Blog*, 15 November [retrieved from: http://blogs.lse.ac.uk/impactofsocialsciences/2011/11/15/world-bank-dissemination].

Orwell, G. (1946) Politics and the English Language, *The Orwell Prize* [retrieved from: https://www.theorwellprize.co.uk/the-orwell-prize/orwell/essays-and-other-works/politics-and-the-english-language/].

Quinn, K. (2011) Jaspan launches The Conversation, *The Age*, 25 March [retrieved from: http:// www.theage.com.au/victoria/jaspan-launches-the-conversation-20110325-1c99v.html].

The Conversation (2017a) *Our Charter* [retrieved from: https://theconversation.com/uk/ charter].

The Conversation (2017b) *Republishing guidelines* [retrieved from: https://theconversation. com/uk/republishing-guidelines].

Viner, K. (2016) How technology disrupted the truth, *The Guardian*, 12 July [retrieved from: https://www.theguardian.com/media/2016/jul/12/how-technology-disrupted-the-truth].

6

Smartphones and tablets: gather new forms of data and create your own apps

Natalia Kucirkova

Introduction

Compact multimedia technologies such as tablets and smartphones offer new, powerful ways to make research ideas visible and accessible. The fact that tablets and smartphones are nowadays used among all sections of the population in many western societies (Common Sense Media, 2013; Formby, 2014), including low-income groups (Smith, 2013), means that the tool for data collection is no different from an everyday object, used by the research participants and researchers. This makes data collection less intrusive and less costly. In addition, the combination of an audio-recorder, video camera, and typewriter within one device lets researchers gather multimedia data in a more seamless and time-efficient way than would be possible with single-function technologies.

A tablet or smartphone can act as an object of research (e.g. researching the use of tablets among youngsters) as well as a tool for data collection (i.e. collecting data with the inbuilt camera, microphone, video, and notepad). It can also be used for research dissemination (e.g. through iBooks) and provision of already transcribed data (with apps that contain built-in diagnostics). As such, extra time demands on researchers engaged in multiple roles can be decreased by taking the opportunity to gather feedback from within the device.

In Chapter 10, Christian Payne describes how to use tablets and smartphones to create engaging videos that can boost researchers' profile and engage wider audiences in research conversation. In this chapter, I outline how you can use tablets and smartphones to gather new forms of data and represent research concepts with apps – that is, software programs for smartphones and tablets. I will also look at ways in which you can apply this knowledge to the actual making of apps and software programs.

Which tablet or smartphone?

Tablets and smartphones (e.g. iPhones, Samsung's Galaxy, the LG or HTC) come with powerful cameras, which can capture detailed, colourful shots. The capabilities of the individual models are improved on a regular basis, so if you are thinking of purchasing a new phone for the purpose of shooting high-quality video, it's best to check a recent review that compares different models currently on offer. Several bloggers regularly review and compare smartphones in relation to their cameras.

Using your own phone or tablet for research purposes

If you use your own smartphone or tablet for research purposes, remember that you need to comply with the ethical requirements for secure data storage and transfer. Password-protected university equipment might be a better option for security reasons. Also, if you are worried about the device getting lost and damaged, most universities can provide short- or long-term insurance. This kind of insurance can typically also cover equipment that is rented or loaned.

First steps: a video protocol

Once you have your equipment ready for data collection, it's time to decide on the video protocol and data you want to record for your project. Given the ease and low cost of recording with digital cameras, you don't need to be as restrictive as researchers used to be in days gone by. However, there is also no point in recording and gathering data that you will not analyse. A video protocol should be written in response to your research aims and objectives. A good video protocol should also include instructions on how and where you want to store your videos and a clear labelling path (typically in the format of project name–date–short description of the picture/video), so that you can easily locate the files and share them with other research team members.

Extra video data documenting the research process

In addition to collecting data that address your research questions, you can also use the camera to document the actual research process. Video is great to capture the research process by recording short vlogs of, for example, the different sites of data collection you might visit, your own thought process as you revise your research questions, or – if you have the participants' consent – some extra contextual data (e.g. participants' informal learning practices if your main research interest is in formal learning). All these extra data can help your analysis later on.

Capturing on-screen activities

If your research is about the use of technologies, then smartphones and tablets offer some exciting options for recording participants' engagement not only around, but also on the screen. With software programs such as Camtasia™, you can record the activity on users' screens as they engage with a specific game, website or image. In addition to commercial software for screen recording, there are also research-based programs, such as the 'obserware app' developed at the University of Waikato. The display recording tool allows researchers to capture not only what happens on the screen, but also more details on the user engagement. For instance, Professor Falloon and colleagues used the display recording tool to capture children's engagement with iPad apps in the class-room. The software recorded children's haptic engagement with various apps (e.g. how long and where children tapped on different hotspots in the apps), as well as the duration and frequency of their engagement with specific parts of the software. The display recording tool is unique in that it allows researchers to see children's engagement on the screen in real time and provides a detailed log of their engagement for later analysis.

If you are interested in documenting users' everyday use of apps and tablets/ smartphones, then you could use so-called tablet spying software (e.g. Appmia™), which lets you record all activities with and around a specific device. For instance, for the purpose of knowing how teenagers interact with social media and their digital devices in informal environments, you could record their activity on social media apps such as WhatsApp, as well as keep track and log of all their calls, the emails they send and receive. If you decide to use any of these embedded covert data-capturing software, you need to be very careful about the ethical implications [check the Ethical Guidelines at the Public Engagement website for more details: https://www.publicengagement.ac.uk/work-with-us/completed-projects/ethics-cbpr/ethical-guidelines-resources]. Your research participants need to know and understand when, where, and for how long they are being recorded and how their data will be stored and used. For vulnerable groups such as young children and people with special learning or educational needs, obtaining informed consent is a challenge, particularly for this kind of data. Remember that as an ethical researcher, you need to adhere to strict ethical principles of social sciences research (see, for example, the Statement of Ethical Practice by the British Sociological Association [http://www.britsoc.co.uk/the-bsa/equality/statement-of-ethical-practice.aspx] and it will depend on the nature and value of each individual research project whether ethical permission can be granted. It is best to discuss your plans with the University Ethics Committee and with the participants and/or their caregivers/guardians before you start collecting data in this way.

Sharing your research video story

Video, photographs or audio recordings taken by smartphone/tablet can enrich your empirical data and help with data analysis. In addition, you can use the multimedia to complement your research dissemination. For the latter, you can create a short video 'research story' summarizing your research aims and findings, and release it on YouTube or Vimeo. A research story can showcase some of your data (e.g. chil-dren using apps in the classroom) or document your research journey. Research stories can be a great way to pique others' interest in your research and acknowledge diverse contributions to a research project. You can also create a video podcast, with a series of short video clips providing an in-depth look into your research.

Whatever you decide, keep in mind that before releasing parts of your data on public platforms such as YouTube, you must check with the participants and your research funder that they are comfortable with you doing so. Typically, research funders and journal publishers encourage their authors to produce a short video research story. For instance, SAGE Knowledge [http://sk.sagepub.com/], the largest social sciences platform showcasing video content, actively encourages SAGE authors to share their findings in a video format.

Analysing video data

Your theoretical framework will determine the ways in which you decide to analyse your video data. If you do social science research and you like using multimodal methods, you might find useful the tips and techniques put together by MODE (the Visual and Multimodal Research Forum for academic discussion on multimodality at the Institute of Education in London). The MODE site [https://mode.ioe.ac.uk/] contains a free online course that will teach you multimodal methods for analysing communication and learning with digital technologies (e.g. video analysis of face-to-face interaction or moving image and digital film production).

As for data visualization and data annotation, several software programs are designed for audio/video editing and processing. You can of course annotate your videos by simply placing them into clearly named folders, cutting them into shorter segments using Windows Media Maker available on any computer/laptop (or iMovie for Mac users) and describing the video segments in a separate Word document. If, however, you would rather have the video with text description in one file, with clearly marked time stamps and annotations, then consider the use of software programs such as MAXQDA™. MAXQDA is a professional research software for qualitative and mixed methods research, which allows you to combine video, audio, and transcript data into one rich file. You can add codes to specific data segments and run simple statistics on them. Unlike NVivo™, which is only for textual data (such as interviews, open-ended survey responses, articles, social media and web content), MAXQDA can combine several formats together.

Audio research stories

With all the focus on video, it might be easy to overlook the value of audio material in engaging research audiences and documenting the research process. Audio can be an accessible way of presenting research to those who are visually impaired or do not want to watch videos for other personal reasons. Provision of sub-titles and transcripts can increase access.

First steps: what to audio record?

You can create an audio research story with some authentic sounds (e.g. excerpts from interviews with your research participants, background noises from the playground if your research is about children), with a voiceover summarizing your main research findings. There are hundreds of audio-recording apps for smartphones and tablets, with various options for editing the finished file. You can achieve great results by simply using the native audio-recording app, which comes with most smartphones and tablets. Make sure your audio recording is clear and easily understood, but don't worry about it being completely professional – it is, after all, the content that matters in this case.

Sharing your audio story

It is likely that your university or the Students Union based at your university runs an official radio channel. There may also be some existing research groups that run their own radio channel or audio podcasts on a regular basis. Reach out to them and ask them if they would like to share your audio research story to raise awareness of your project and of the university research activities.

Alternatively, you can create your own podcast channel on one of the freely available domains such as iTunes, soundcloud.com or YouTube. Audio podcasts are a great way not only to disseminate your research findings in a flexible format, but also to create a forum and online meeting space for like-minded researchers. For example, you could have a podcast channel dedicated to children's hearing problems or science fieldwork projects or Shakespeare's literature. There are as many options as there are research topics. If your subject is a niche area, a podcast channel can make it more visible and create a space for other researchers to connect around the topic.

If you host your audios on a public website, you can reach a more diverse audiences than through a university channel but you will need to spend more time on raising awareness about its existence (e.g. cross-advertising on academia.edu or ResearchGate and sharing regular updates through blogs and Twitter). Remember, these online spaces are a great way to create opportunities for discussion and debate.

Tablets and smartphones not only offer new ways for gathering data but also for creating new products – apps.

App development for everyday use or research purposes

In addition to testing, evaluating, and documenting apps' use, researchers can also create their own apps (Kucirkova, 2016). Several scholars and research groups have done so. For research purposes, you can create apps that facilitate data collection and insight into the research process. For example, an iPad app for promoting numeracy skills was created at the University of Gothenburg in 2012 by Barendregt and colleagues. The app can record the number of successful and failed answers but also more general patterns of use (e.g. location of tapping). Thus, while children are having fun with a mathematics app, researchers can be collecting data on the history and pattern of use of individual users without the need for an intrusive mechanism.

Other researchers have created apps that not only help their research process, but have also become everyday tools used by people at large. For instance, a research group at the University of Liverpool led by Dr. Eric Robinson created a weight loss app as part of their obesity research. Computer scientists from the University of California San Diego have developed their own app, ProtectMyPrivacy, which notifies users when their personal information is at risk. And researchers from the University of Cambridge have developed an app that guesses which part of England you are from based on your accent. Perhaps one day there will be an app accompanying every research topic.

First steps: creating an app

One way to create an app is to collaborate with those who know how to do it – app developers. Although partnerships between app developers and academics are still rare, there are more and more examples of apps co-produced in consultation or partnership with academics, especially in the education domain. For instance, the iLearn apps from Toca Boca studio have been developed through academic partnerships with educational researchers and childhood psychologists at McGill University in Montreal.

Another way of developing your app is to take stock of the expertise of app development at your university. Most universities will have at least one in-house app developer who might be able to bring your idea to life. This was the case when I did my PhD at The Open University and developed the Our Story app.

My experience of designing the Our Story app

In 2011, at a time when iPads and iPad apps were just emerging on the educational market, I was researching personalization and shared book reading as part of my postgraduate degree at The Open University in the UK. I was interested to find new and innovative ways to encourage parents and children to share stories together, and to create a story based on their personal experience. I worked closely with parents of 3–5-year-old children with whom I co-created so-called personalized books. These books were laminated paper books containing the parents' and children's pictures, drawings, and texts.

In order to create such personalized books, we needed to print out the pictures, cut them out, stick them to cardboard, add the text, and laminate the books. Although this was an enjoyable process, it was very time-consuming and required many costly re-makes (e.g. some pictures just didn't look good when printed out, some captions needed to be rewritten for legibility, lamination fell apart, etc.). There was also the limitation of only one copy of each book, which meant limited possibilities to share with others.

Mindful of these limitations and of the rising popularity of apps and digital books for young children, the idea of a book-creation app arose. Initially, the app 'Our Story' was designed for 3–5-year-old children, who could use it at home together with their parents. I spent countless hours with the university app designer discussing the app user interface and mechanisms of use. My PhD supervisors, Professors Messer and Sheehy, provided advice and recommendations from their child psychology perspective; several other colleagues at the university commented on the app's design and functionalities. We also asked groups of children, parents, and teachers for their ideas on design improvement and refined the app according to their feedback. To ensure that the app was compatible with all devices, we created a version for Apple and Android devices (today you can use coding language compatible with any platform).

Once the app was available for download from the Googlemarket and Apple app store, we tested and evaluated its use with parents and their children at home, as well as in primary and early years classrooms. Teachers were particularly helpful in suggesting further design improvements and inventing many creative uses of the app.

Although initially designed for parent–child story-making, the app has been re-purposed for creating personalized stories and to support the learning of the English, history, and mathematics curricula (see Kucirkova, 2014). Design changes in the past few years have included additional printing options (we added several sizes enabling A4-, A5-, and A6-sized booklets as well as possibilities for short video stories and templates).

Since its public launch, Our Story has been used in research projects across the world including Spain, Japan, the USA, Taiwan, and the UK (Scotland and England). In addition to children of pre-school age, the app is a popular resource for children with special educational needs as well as elderly people with dementia who can work particularly well with an iconic, colour-coded, simple user-interface. The main design of Our Story (a gallery of pictures on the top and a filmstrip down the bottom) has been emulated by many commercially available story-making apps, evidencing the impact a research-based app can have on the designer community. The range of research projects documenting the app's benefits for various groups of children illustrates the influence a research-based app can have on children's literacy and language development.

Independent development of apps

If you decide to produce an app on your own and if you are new to coding and programming, then check out the App Inventor, developed at Massachusetts Institute of Education. The App Inventor is a visual programming tool that allows users of even very limited IT knowledge to create their own apps. The site guides you through coding in a few simple steps. Text-based coding is replaced with a visual drag-and-drop system. This means that experienced users can create a suite of fully functioning apps within a few hours and those who are completely new to app design can easily create their first app.

If you wish to make your app commercially available or release it as a free resource in one of the official app stories, you need to have a developer account. Setting up a developer account for Android or Apple devices is not difficult, but it is not free, so you might need to include these expenses in your research plan. You will need to comply with the design and user guidelines before either of the platforms accepts your product.

Whichever approach to app development you decide to take, remember that apps, just like any software are time-bound, their capabilities will need to evolve as the hardware evolves, and that requires time and financial commitment. So that your app doesn't soon become obsolete, you need to budget some time and money for regular upgrades and bug fixing. Seen from a positive point of view, app updates can be used as an opportunity to re-connect to your audience, remind them of your research and newest findings. For instance, you can use your app to push notifications to its users and embed short surveys into them, gauging timely user-feedback. On the other hand, curating an app is often a challenging process with the app stores dictating their own rules. If, for example, Apple releases a new software update and your app is not compatible with it, you will need to cover the cost of the app's update.

Example from Practice

Partnerships between researchers and app designers are not yet the norm, but some exceptions exist. For instance, Professor Rvachew and colleagues from McGill University collaborated with the app producer Triba Nova. The apps they co-created are based on the famous Caillou stories and are called iRead With (the 'with' illustrating the emphasis on shared reading experiences). Unlike many children's digital books, iRead With encourages the shared active reading experience of a parent and child, based on Rvachew and colleagues' research on the importance of shared reading in families (Rees et al., 2017).

Common Pitfalls

- Although apps offer unprecedented possibilities for capturing user data, researchers need to be wary of novel ethical challenges represented by collecting detailed personal information in a manner that is not always transparent to the user.
- Be wary of the cost implications of software such as MAXQDA at the design stages of your project. Think through how you want to collect and analyse your data and budget in all extra software and hardware equipment needed at all stages of the research.
- The design of apps is not only about designing and releasing the app, it is also about curating the app and ensuring it is compatible with the latest software.

Best Practice

- Clear ethical consent forms for collecting and sharing multimedia material are essential for saving you time later in the research process.
- The best apps are those that are developed iteratively and with input from various user groups.
- When collaborating with practitioners and designers in app production, it is important to be clear about everyone's value to and motivation for the project. As clichéd as it may sound, a shared vision of the final product is essential for the project to be successful.

Cited resources

App Inventor [http://appinventor.mit.edu/explore/]
Appmia™ [https://appmia.com/]
Camtasia™ [https://www.techsmith.com/video-editor.html]
MAXQDA™ [http://www.maxqda.com/]
NVivo™ [http://www.qsrinternational.com/what-is-nvivo]
Our Story app [http://www.open.ac.uk/creet/main/projects/our-story]

References

Barendregt, W., Lindström, B., Rietz-Leppänen, E., Holgersson, I. and Ottosson, T. (2012) Development and evaluation of Fingu: a mathematics iPad game using multitouch interaction, in *IDC 2012* (pp. 1–4), 12–15 June, Bremen.

Common Sense Media (2013) *Zero to Eight: Children's media use in America 2013*. San Francisco, CA: Common Sense Media.

Formby, S. (2014) *Practitioner Perspectives: Children's use of technology in the early years*. London: National Literacy Trust.

Kucirkova, N. (2014) *iPads and Tablets in the Classroom: Personalising children's stories*. Leicester: UKLA.

Kucirkova, N. (2016) iRPD – a framework for guiding design-based research with iPad apps, *British Journal of Educational Technology*, 48(2): 598–610 [doi: 10.1111/bjet.12389].

Rees, K., Nadig, A. and Rvachew, S. (2017) Story-related discourse by parent–child dyads: a comparison of typically developing children and children with language impairments, *International Journal of Child–Computer Interaction*, 12: 16–23.

Smith, A. (2013) *Smartphone ownership 2013*. Washington, DC: Pew Research Center [retrieved from: http://www.pewinternet.org/2013/06/05/smartphone-ownership-2013/].

Scholarship in the information age: representing identity, accessing information

Nicola Dowson

Introduction

The mainstreaming of the internet in the late 1990s offered the potential to increase the visibility, discoverability, and accessibility of research outputs both within and outside of academia. Over the last two decades there has been a shift by publishers and researchers to provide resources online that can be accessed asynchronously from anywhere with an internet connection.

In the first half of this chapter, I provide an overview of developments and tools that enable researchers to represent their research online and build their online research profile. In the second half of the chapter, I give a brief overview of digital and information literacy skills required by twenty-first-century researchers and the current information landscape. I then outline tools and techniques that can assist researchers in navigating the plethora of online resources that are now available and potentially save time in locating information. I also offer advice on how to evaluate information and include an overview of tools that can help with the effective management of your search results.

Representing identity

Developments in scholarly communication

The connected world that we live in has made it increasingly important for researchers to build and maintain their online profiles and alongside this disseminate their research findings both within and outside of their academic communities. Building and maintaining your research profile can help raise awareness of your research, increase its readership, and enable you to establish research networks. Open access publishing, which was embraced by the science community in the 1990s, has become more widespread over the last few years, especially in the UK and Europe where it has become a requirement of funders of research. There are two colours of open access:

- *Gold*: Where the final version of a publication is made freely available immediately via the publisher's website. This usually involves the payment of an article processing charge (APC) to the publisher by the author/authors or the authors' institution. In 2012, the British government instigated a Working Group on Expanding Access to Published Research Findings. Their final report (Finch, 2012) made a number of recommendations that were accepted by the government. These included that there should be policy direction towards immediate open access, through the payment of APCs.
- *Green*: Where a full-text version of the publication is made available via an institutional or subject repository. Depending on the version (for example, pre-print, authors' accepted manuscript, version of record), the publisher may stipulate an embargo on the full text being freely downloadable. Most institutional repositories offer a 'request a copy' feature, which facilitates the author sharing a personal copy with an individual. Open Research Online (ORO), the Open University's (UK) repository of research outputs, received just under 1.3 million downloads of open access items in 2015–2016 (The Orb, 2016). A study of open access papers at Chalmers University of Technology in Sweden found that 'self-archived articles had a 22% higher citation rate than those that weren't archived' (Kullman, 2014).

Alongside developments in open access publishing, there has been a growth in academic social networking sites such as Academia.edu and ResearchGate. The primary focus of these was to enable researchers to establish an online profile and to support the building of research communities. Google Scholar also offers the functionality to set up a personal profile. In addition, academic social networking sites enable the sharing of research outputs via either uploading of the full text or individuals requesting a copy from the author. If you plan to share the full text of your article through social networking sites, it is advisable to check the contract you signed with the publisher and your publisher's archiving policy first, as this action could potentially contravene certain obligations in the contract that you signed. If in doubt you should ask your publisher for advice before sharing.

Institutional and subject repositories and academic social networking sites are of benefit to researchers without an institutional affiliation, as they may not have access to the subscription resources that are traditionally paid for by an institution's library.

Funders and publishers are moving towards requiring research data to be made available alongside the publications to enable re-use. There are now a growing number of platforms where research data can be accessed, including Figshare (multidisciplinary research data), UK Data Archive (social sciences and humanities research data), UK Data Service (social, economic, and population data resources) and Zenodo (multi-disciplinary research data). The Registry of

Research Data Repositories [http://www.re3data.org/] is a global registry of research data repositories covering all disciplines. When re-using research data, it is important that you look at the licence to see what re-use (if any) is permitted.

Holliman (2010: 1) observed that 'social media provide opportunities to communicate in more immediate and informal ways, while digital technologies have the potential to make the various processes of research more visible in the public sphere'.

There are a number of digital tools that facilitate the dissemination of research. Blogs are an established form of scholarly communication and offer the potential for researchers to share, provide updates, and receive comment and feedback on their research in a less formal way. Most blogs offer the option of subscribing to RSS (Really Simple Syndication) feeds or email alerts of new content, potentially saving time in having to visit a number of blogs to see if any new content has been added. A word of caution, it is easy to set up alerts and become overwhelmed with emails that you do not have time to follow up, so it is important to regularly review the email alerts that you receive and unsubscribe to any that are not adding value to your research. Wordpress, one of the most popular blogging platforms, has the facility to set up an account that enables you to manage your Wordpress blog subscriptions from one place.

Twitter, a microblogging tool that was launched in 2006, can be useful for disseminating open access research outputs. However, for this to be an effective conduit of research output, you will need to build your followers. Many publisher platforms are set up to enable comments and feedback to be received from the research community and beyond, extending the peer-review of manuscripts and enabling new insights to be given. And the *Handbook of Social Media for Researchers and Supervisors* (Minocha and Petre, 2012) includes a section on tips for social networking for research dialogues and guidance notes for a range of social media tools.

All researchers need to ensure that their publications are attributed to their personal profiles. ORCID is a 16-digit unique identifier that enables you to claim your research publications and distinguishes you from every researcher in the world. ORCID advise that you include your ORCID id on individual webpages, when you submit publications to a publisher, and on external funding applications.

In his open access book, *The Battle for Open*, Martin Weller comments: 'open scholarship offers new opportunities and tensions for individuals, and one means of examining these is to consider the concept of academic identity' (Weller, 2014: 140), and notes that researchers need to give some consideration to openness and decide how best it works for them.

Accessing information

Digital and information literacy

Information literacy skills have always been a core competency required by researchers. The ability to find, evaluate, and use information and navigate the

Common Pitfalls

- Not managing and maintaining your research identity and profile.
- Setting up blogs and Twitter accounts and not utilizing them.
- Not utilizing services offered through your academic institution. For example, depositing the full text of your publications on an institutional repository.

Best Practice

- Claim your research by registering for an ORCID.
- Consider which social media and social networking sites meet your research identity needs.
- Consider how open you wish your research outputs to be and base your decision where to publish on this.
- If you work at an academic institution, utilize services that will assist with dissemination of your research. For example, deposit the full text of your publications on an institutional repository.

digital world we live in are essential research skills. In 2011, the Society of College, National and University Libraries (SCONUL) developed seven pillars of information literacy as a core model for higher education. This model 'defines core skills and competencies (ability) and attitudes and behaviours (understanding) at the heart of information literacy development in higher education' (SCONUL, 2011). The seven pillars are 'identify, scope, plan, gather, evaluate, manage and present' (SCONUL, 2011). The UK's Vitae Researcher Development Framework 'has been developed by and for researchers working in higher education as an aid to planning, promoting and enhancing professional development' (Vitae, 2012). This framework includes an information literacy lens (Vitae, 2012) that provides a bridge between it and the seven pillars of information literacy. This information literacy lens 'provides an overview of the key knowledge, behaviours and attributes that can be acquired through, or used in, information literacy activities' (Vitae, 2012). The lens can be used to articulate information literacy skills you already have and identify areas that you would like to develop.

Online databases and discovery tools

Online databases aggregate content and enable cross-searching of content in a number of different ways – by keyword, author or title, for example. Many databases offer additional functionality, such as saving searches so they can be re-run, setting up search alerts, bookmarking, and emailing search results. It is always worth spending time reviewing a database's help pages to see what additional functionality is available.

Although many publisher databases require a subscription to access the content, there are a growing number of open access databases that are free to access. Examples include:

- ArXiv – an open access subject repository covering physics, mathematics, computer science, quantitative biology, quantitative finance and statistics.
- COnnecting REpositories (CORE) – aggregates and enables cross-searching of open access full-text content on institutional repositories.
- Directory of Open Access Books – an online directory that indexes and provides access to peer-reviewed open access books.
- Directory of Open Access Journals (DOAJ) – an online directory that indexes and provides access to high-quality, open access, peer-reviewed journals.
- Google Scholar – a web search engine that indexes a range of content and provides full-text access to some of it. There is a library links option that enables you to gain seamless access to your institution's library (if the library has enabled this facility) from within Google Scholar.

If you are working or studying at a university, your library can advise you on relevant databases in your field. For researchers without a university affiliation, public and national libraries can be a source of advice.

Discovery tools enable the cross-searching of a number of resources at the same time, therefore saving both time and effort and many university libraries provide access to these. They can provide a starting point for identifying relevant databases in your subject area.

It is important to bear in mind that in the digital world these search engines and discovery tools may change over time and some may disappear completely. Therefore, it is important not to be reliant on just one source for your information needs and to spend some time keeping up to date and evaluating new tools that have emerged.

Search techniques and tips

Searching for information takes time. Planning and preparation prior to undertaking your searches can save you time and effort.

To carry out a thorough information search, it is wise to spend time compiling a list of relevant search terms. This requires you to define your research questions and think about what type of information you need. Think about synonyms, related terms, and different spellings of words (e.g. British English and American English spellings). Keyword and descriptors used in journal articles can be useful in identifying relevant search terms. Some databases have a list of subject terms you can review when deciding which keywords to use in your search. And check if the resource you are searching supports phrase searching, which will enable you to search for the exact words in the order specified. This is particularly useful if the research community is using a common phrase to describe a particular phenomenon.

When carrying out searches, Boolean logic allows you to link search terms together in specific ways and enables either narrowing or broadening of your search. Using Boolean logic allows you to search more precisely, ensuring the search captures relevant results. When searching a database, you may notice that Boolean operators are built into the search options; in some databases, you will find them within the advanced search options.

The Boolean operators are AND, OR, and NOT:

- AND narrows your search results, as both words need to be found in the returned results. This is useful when you have carried out a search and it has returned a large number of results. It is also useful if you want to find information on a particular aspect of a subject. For example, smartphones AND education.
- OR broadens your search by returning results for one of the search terms or both of them. This is useful when you have carried out a search and it has returned only a small number of results, or when you are using synonyms or related words and want to ensure both are returned in the results. For example, smartphones OR mobile phones.
- NOT narrows your search by excluding terms. This is useful when you are using a broad search term but want to exclude a particular aspect of a subject that may be returned in your search results. For example, smartphones NOT tablets.

In some databases, you can use a symbol to search different forms of a word. With truncation, for example, which is useful when searching for the singular and plural of a word or when searching for terms that can be reduced to a common stem, an asterisk (*) is normally used. For example, searching for skill* would give search results containing the keywords skill, skills, skilling, skilled, etc. Some databases also offer a 'wildcard' search functionality, and here the symbol is usually either a question mark (?) or hash (#). Wildcards are useful for searching for both American and British spellings. For example, searching for behavio?r will retrieve search results that include behaviour and behavior, while searching cultur# will give search results that start with cultur, including culture, cultural, and culturally.

Most databases have the facility to limit your search to particular date ranges or periods, which is useful if you want to narrow your search results and look for material published or written in a particular period. It is worth bearing in mind that it may take a while for articles to be published, so although you may search and locate a recent paper, the research behind it may have been carried out some time previously. There may also be functionality to limit searches to geographical areas or a particular language.

Some databases offer a Cited References or Citation Searching facility, such as Thomson Reuters Web of Science (which includes the Arts and Humanities, Social Sciences and Science Citation Index) and Google Scholar. This enables you to do a search for a particular paper and find more recent papers that have cited this article. Elsevier's Scopus database has a 'set citation alert' option that allows you to set up an email alert which informs you when an article is cited in Scopus. Related Records is another feature offered by some databases (e.g. Web of Science), which returns a list of articles related to the article that you have found.

A database's help pages provide an overview of its searching functionality and tips on searching the database. If you are using a database you are not familiar with or if you want to fine-grain your search results, it is always worth spending time reviewing the help material to get an overview of the searching functionality available.

Evaluating your search results

Once you have completed your search, it is important to evaluate the information you have found to ensure it is relevant and meets your needs.

Library Services at the Open University in the UK developed the PROMPT criteria (The Open University, 2014). This is a framework that can be used to evaluate your search results. PROMPT stands for Presentation, Relevance, Objectivity, Method, Provenance, and Timeliness. Below is a brief overview of each of the criteria:

- Presentation – the way that information is presented has an effect on how we receive and perceive it. If the presentation is poor and the language is not clear, it makes the academic content difficult to critically evaluate.
- Relevance – is the information you have found relevant to the research question you want to answer? Things to consider include geographical location (do you want information about a particular area or country?) and level of the information (e.g. is it too general or too detailed for your needs?).
- Objectivity – this encompasses developing a critical awareness of the research in your area and the different positions and views that are represented. Look to see if the author clearly states their viewpoint. Opinion can sometimes be stated as fact, so look for evidence in the information provided that would substantiate any facts. Language can give an indication of objectivity, for example, vague language may indicate that the findings are not robust.
- Method – using your knowledge of the methods adopted in your subject area, review the publication to identify if it is clear how the research was carried out and whether the methods were appropriate.
- Provenance – can you easily identify the author, sponsoring body or source of your information? Things to consider include where the information has been published (e.g. a peer-reviewed journal or grey literature). Is the author an acknowledged expert in the subject area? What type of organization is sponsoring the research and does it have any vested interest in the subject area being researched?

- Timeliness – it is important that you think about your information need in relation to when the information was produced. Things to consider include whether you need the most up-to-date information, and is the information you have found still current or has it been superseded?

You may find it useful to take a pick-and-mix approach to using the PROMPT criteria to evaluate your search results, or you may consider that some of the criteria above are more relevant than others when undertaking the evaluation.

Managing your search results and information

Managing your search results and the publications that you have found during your search is an important part of the research process. There are a number of bibliographic and reference management tools that can help you organize and manage your search results. Many of these are freely available (e.g. EndNote Basic, Mendeley, RefMe, Zotero) and allow the transfer of search results from a range of databases into them, saving the researcher time in having to manually key in or copy and paste information.

Most offer the facility to save PDFs alongside the bibliographic information of the publication and enable the tagging of publications by keyword and the facility to add your own notes that can make retrieval at a later date much easier. Some allow the setting up of groups so you can share search results and publications you have found with others. Some may also recommend relevant publications to you based on the research outputs you are saving in them.

Bibliographic and reference management tools also support referencing and you can use them in Word and Open Office to create in-text citations and bibliographies in a range of output styles. They can also save you time, though you do have to invest some time initially in learning how to use them.

These tools are rapidly evolving and new functionality is continuously being added, so it is worth regularly reviewing what new functionality is available. Many have online support forums and networks that offer a good source of help and advice.

Example from Practice

I am starting to research on the use of smartphones and education. This is a broad area, so I decide that I want to focus on Higher Education. I carry out a search using the keywords 'smartphone?' AND 'Higher Education'. I want to find the most recent articles, so limit my search to research outputs published after 2014. Finally, after briefly looking at some of the results, I decide I do not want publications on tablets so I search for 'smartphone?' AND 'Higher Education' NOT tablet?. Again, I limit my research results to those published after 2014.

Common Pitfalls

- Starting searching without developing a search strategy and thinking about what keywords to search for. Some advanced planning can potentially save time and effort and give you better results.
- Having a number of 'known' sources that you use to find information. You may be missing out on relevant results, so do take time to keep abreast of new resources and new forms of scholarly communication in your subject discipline.
- Not exploiting bibliographic and reference management tools to manage your research results.

Best Practice

- Develop a search strategy and think about what are the relevant keywords for your research question.
- Review the help pages of the databases and resources you are searching to ensure you are utilizing their full functionality.
- Setting up email alerts can help you keep abreast of new publications and developments in your discipline – but make sure you manage these and unsubscribe to any that you are not looking at.
- Abstracts are useful for quickly evaluating the relevance of a publication to your research question. For more detailed evaluation, consider using the PROMPT Framework (The Open University, 2014).
- Consider investing the time in learning how to use a bibliographic or reference management tool. This will enable you to build an online catalogue of relevant information and resources throughout your research career and beyond.

Cited resources

Academia.edu [https://www.academia.edu/]
ArXiv [https://arxiv.org/]
COnnecting REpositories (CORE) [https://core.ac.uk/]
Directory of Open Access Books [http://www.doabooks.org/]
Directory of Open Access Journals [https://doaj.org/]
EndNote Basic [http://endnote.com/product-details/basic]
Figshare [https://figshare.com/]
Google Scholar [http://scholar.google.co.uk/]
Mendeley [https://www.mendeley.com/]
Open Research Online (ORO) [http://oro.open.ac.uk]
ORCID [http://orcid.org/]
RefMe [https://www.refme.com/uk/]
Registry of Research Data Repositories [http://www.re3data.org/]

ResearchGate [https://www.researchgate.net/]
Twitter [http://www.twitter.com]
UK Data Archive [http://www.data-archive.ac.uk/]
UK Data Service [https://www.ukdataservice.ac.uk/]
Zenodo [https://zenodo.org/]
Zotero [https://www.zotero.org/]

References

Finch, J. (2012) *Accessibility, Sustainability, Excellence: How to expand access to research publications*. Report of the Working Group on Expanding Access to Published Research Findings [retrieved from: https://www.acu.ac.uk/research-information-network/finch-report-final].

Holliman, R. (2010) From analogue to digital scholarship: implications for science communication researchers, *Journal of Science Communication*, 9 (3): 1–6 [retrieved from: https://jcom.sissa.it/archive/09/03/Jcom0903(2010)C01/Jcom0903(2010)C05].

Kullman, L. (2104) The effect of open access on citation rates of self-archived articles at Chalmers, *IATUL 35th Annual Conference*, Aalto University, Espoo, Finland, 2–5 June 2014 [retrieved from: http://publications.lib.chalmers.se/records/fulltext/198512/local_198512.pdf].

Minocha, S. and Petre, M. (2012) *Handbook of Social Media for Researchers and Supervisors*. Vitae Innovate/The Open University [retrieved from: http://oro.open.ac.uk/34271/1/Vitae-Innovate-Open-University-Social-Media-Handbook-2012.pdf].

SCONUL (2011) *The SCONUL seven pillars of information literacy: core model for higher education* [retrieved from: http://www.sconul.ac.uk/sites/default/files/documents/coremodel.pdf].

The Open University (2014) *Advanced evaluation using PROMPT* [retrieved from: http://www.open.ac.uk/libraryservices/documents/advanced-evaluation-using-prompt.pdf].

The Orb (2016) *ORO Annual Report* [retrieved from: http://www.open.ac.uk/blogs/the_orb/?p=1486].

Vitae (2012) *Information literacy lens on the Vitae Researcher Development Framework 2012* [retrieved from: https://www.vitae.ac.uk/vitae-publications/rdf-related/information-literacy-lens-on-the-vitae-researcher-development-framework-rdf-apr-2012.pdf].

Weller, M. (2014) *The Battle for Open*. London: Ubiquity Press.

Developing a distinctive digital profile and network

John J. Oliver

Introduction

'What do you want to be when you grow up?' This is a common question and one that you have probably not heard since your formative years. However, in a world increasingly disrupted by digital technologies, experienced academics are (or at least should be) asking themselves how they adapt to the new digital landscape. Early career academics, on the other hand, will be looking at the opportunities that digital technology can offer them to develop their profile, access new networks, and extend the reach and impact of their research outputs. So, the question is not so much about 'What do you want to be when you grow up?' as 'What type of academic do you want to be in the digital world?'

In this chapter, I look at some of the key questions that academics of all ages need to address, before focusing on how they can develop a distinctive academic profile that will enable them to connect with, and make the most of, the network opportunities that are available to them in a digital landscape. To paraphrase Ahmed and Olander (2012), in a world gone digital, it doesn't matter who you were or how good you were yesterday, the digital world means that you need to recalibrate, set a new direction, understand the metrics that matter, and multiply your contribution to academic knowledge and practice.

Recalibrating and setting the direction

There is an old adage: if you fail to plan, then you plan to fail. In setting the broad context for this discussion, researchers need to consider several strategic questions about their long-term objectives and the resources and capabilities required to meet those objectives. Put simply, you need a plan. If this all sounds too prescriptive, then think again, the digitally agile researcher cannot afford to sit back and wait for things to happen. The competition for jobs, funding applications, and access to internal training funds is fierce and looks set only to intensify in an age of market-driven higher education where phrases like 'return on investment' are increasingly being used in academic circles. Thus, if you want to create a strong digital presence and network, taking the time to think things through and making a plan is an essential part of the career development process.

For the most part, an academic career offers a lot of variety and there will be opportunities at certain points to evaluate what you want to do for the next few years going forward. So, whether you are an experienced academic or new to the field, answering three important strategic questions will provide you with a platform on which to develop the next phrase of your career:

- What *type* of academic career do you want?
- What do *you value* in an academic career?
- What do the *institutions* you work for, or plan to work for, value?

The answers to these questions will help you to recalibrate, plan, and set the direction for the next phase of your career. For example, if you believe that you would like a career as an academic who engages and consults with business (i.e. an academic-consultant), then your digital profile would need to emphasize the *relevance and currency* of your research to both academic and professional practice networks. If, on the other hand, you would like to develop a career as an academic-researcher, then your digital profile would need to emphasize the *citation impact* of your work and how your research pushes the boundaries of theoretical knowledge.

It is also fair to say that the type of academic career you have will undoubtedly change over time and be influenced by a number of internal and external factors, such as what motivates you, family, salary, career development opportunities, and location among other things. It is also worth remembering that the university sector in many countries is changing, and increasingly academics are being asked to do more in the same amount of time. The consequence of this could be that *your values* become diluted to a certain extent, but it is important to stay true to what you believe in and what differentiates you in a competitive marketplace.

The key thing to remember is that thinking through the answers to these important questions will help you develop the right type of personal brand and digital profile – and engage effectively with the right networks.

Developing a distinctive digital research profile

The key message here is focus. Hopefully, your self-analysis and answer to the first strategic question, *'What type of academic career do you want?'*, will have helped you set your objectives for the next phase of your career. This self-analysis will also have identified your values, strengths, weaknesses, beliefs, and values as an academic, and it is at this point that you need to think about yourself as a 'brand'. Hood et al. (2014: 34) noted the importance of this concept by arguing that creating a compelling personal brand is an issue of strategic importance and one that helps you to build your online reputation and to effectively position you and your research in the minds of your audiences. Another way of looking at personal branding is to consider how *you* and *your* work would want to be remembered in years to come: your legacy. This may seem an odd thing to do at the start of your career, or indeed at the start of the next phase of your career, but this type of reflective self-analysis will really help you to think about your personal brand. Poeppelman and Blacksmith (2014: 112) drew an interesting personal branding parallel with industrial-organizational psychology, arguing that:

> It's natural to trust what you know. When you walk into a store, you tend to gravitate towards the brands you are familiar with. You know what they provide and you trust what you will get. In the modern global digital world standing out is a tall order.

In order to consider yourself as a brand, you need to think about your values and beliefs and set about creating a narrative about who you are and then telling the digital world about it. Remember, creating a strong personal brand enables you to connect with like-minded researchers and will enable you to situate yourself not only in the right networks, but also in a way that differentiates you within those networks. Poeppelman and Blacksmith (2014: 113) concluded, 'personal branding can benefit each one of us by advancing our own personal growth, career movement, and self-awareness'. Thus, the rewards gained from a strong personal brand and digital presence are certainly worth the effort.

People with strong personal brands tend to specialize in one area of inquiry for a considerable amount of time. Again, it comes back to focus. So, how do you create a strong personal brand? When creating your brand, you need to think about the following questions and make sure that you create an identity and narrative about you and your research:

- What is your objective?
- What differentiates you from other people in your research field?
- What do you have to say that's interesting?
- What new knowledge do you have or are interested in gaining?

If you want a strong personal brand, then you need to create a core message and point of differentiation between you and the rest of your academic peers. So, what is the next step in the personal branding process? Well, we have already considered the strategic importance of self-analysis and the type of academic you would like to be and created a narrative around your brand. The next step is to evaluate your current web presence and your positioning online. This may sound like a difficult process, but actually it's quite straightforward and doesn't take too long to complete. One way to do this is to type in *your name* in Google and see what comes up in the search results. Do you feature on the first page of results, or indeed any page? Then type in the name of your subject field, and then do another search on your specific research area. Thus in three easy steps you will have identified the extent of your online presence, how you are positioned in your subject field, and how much of an impact you and your research are making in the digital landscape. If the results are depressing, then don't despair. This type of 'brand audit' will reveal who the major academic players are in your subject field and how much of an impact their work is having on the subject domain and society in general. These people now need to be considered as *role models*, and you need to think about how you can develop a similar type of digital profile. If, on the other hand, your search results indicate that you do have a web presence, then the thing you now need to do is consider how 'consistent' your profile is across the plethora of digital platforms that are available to researchers. Poeppelman and Blacksmith (2012: 115) noted the importance of having a consistent digital profile when they said that contradictory messages about your personal brand will lead 'people to start questioning the authenticity of your brand promise' and be less inclined to trust and connect with you in the future. In the digital world, this can prove to be time-consuming, since there are many platforms ranging from organizational staff profile pages to academic social networks like Academia.edu, Research Gate, Social Science Research Network, and Google Scholar among many others. It is also worth noting that this consistency in digital profile is important, since online profile descriptions, photographs, and your general appearance often provide the basis for 'social comparisons' (Haferkamp and Krämer, 2011) and can dictate whether or not you will be accepted into some online networks.

Now that you have established your personal brand and set about creating a consistent online personal brand identity, you need to think about your audiences. Who are they and why should they listen to what you have to say? Wetsch (2012: 30) emphasized the importance of 'crafting the correct message' in targeting the right audience, so when you blog or tweet on an issue, make sure that what you say is consistent with your brand and that it reinforces your reputation and point of differentiation. For example, if you are communicating with an academic research community, you need to make sure that you use subject-specific terminology, set your work within existing knowledge, and emphasize that your findings and conclusions are based on a rigorous methodological approach. Alternatively, if you are communicating with a business community, the language should be clear and concise with the information that you are disseminating presented as a series of actionable points. Thus, the message here is that your research outputs need to be tailored for the target audience. One size does not fit all in this case.

Connecting with online networks and disseminating your research to a range of global audiences

The next step is to decide how far you want to extend your digital footprint. North and Oliver (2014: 1) argued that your profile needs to be 'on numerous digital platforms in order to be seen as contemporary and relevant' by stake-holders. There is no doubt that the digital world offers an array of opportunities to extend your digital footprint. However, it can be confusing and having many digital platforms makes it difficult to evaluate which platform you should be on. Thus, you need to think clearly about the reasons for extending your digital footprint across many platforms because, ultimately, being on as many platforms as possible will only end up diluting your core message and add to the time spent on maintaining your profile across these different platforms.

A digital platform is the same as any other medium and for it to be effective you need to think about your audiences first and then the digital platform. As North and Oliver (2014: 1) noted, you need to think about how you can best communicate with and serve your audiences, and

> . . . don't forget what works for your brand, its values and assets. This should be an equally important voice in deciding the digital platform that will help you meet your objective.

For example, if you are an academic-consultant, then LinkedIn and Twitter are excellent platforms to get your message out to the business community, whereas the academic-researcher would need to disseminate their research on academic platforms such as Academia.edu and the Social Science Research Network.

Once you have generated your digital profile and considered the appropriate online platforms that you want to be seen on, you need to think about how you engage with users on these platforms. In their recent article 'Learning to love networking', Casciaro et al. (2016: 104) provide a lucid discussion on the stereo-typical views on networking, saying that some people believe that it

> . . . makes them feel uncomfortable and phony – even dirty. Although some people have a natural passion for it – namely, the extroverts who love and thrive on social interaction – many understandably see it as brown-nosing, exploitative, and inauthentic.

However, they go on to point out that there is a substantial amount of evidence to suggest that people who actively engage in networking activities are far more likely to produce more innovative research and advance their career at the same time. What is interesting in their argument is that researchers who have a natural aversion to networking can overcome this problem by thinking about it differ-ently. Indeed, by creating a mind-set that focuses on identifying other research-ers who have the same common goal and shared interests as you, the 'chore' of networking becomes an activity that will make it 'feel more authentic and mean-ingful' (Casciaro et al., 2016: 107) to you. Uzzi and Dunlap (2005) also noted that these shared interests can create powerful networks that have the potential to create 'high-stakes activities that connect you' with influential players in your subject field.

In the digital world, a lot of networking activity is informal. You can connect, and develop a relationship, using different digital tools and platforms. However, the key to effective networking is to think about it as a 'systematic process' (Byham, 2009) in terms of structure, composition, and engagement.

In terms of *structure*, this point is illustrated extremely well by Ibarra and Hunter (2007) in their article 'How leaders create and use networks'. They argue that your networks need to be configured in three ways in order for them to be effective for you and the other people in those networks. Don't forget, these are social networks, so reciprocal exchange and a win–win for both parties will maximize the benefits in those networks. Ibarra and Hunter (2007) argued that the structure of your network needs to be:

- Operational – where you should build good working relationships with the people that you work most closely with on a day-to-day basis.
- Personal – where you identify like-minded people inside and outside of your organization who can provide you with a stimulus for personal growth and development.
- Strategic – where you develop both horizontal (people who work at the same grade as you) and vertical (people who work at higher grades than you) relationships with people outside of your operational network. These people can provide big picture views and strategic direction on important issues that you face in your operational role and career development.

In terms of network *composition*, you need to consider the people in each of your operational, personal, and strategic networks. Far too often, people consider an effective network to be a numbers game, believing that having 500+ connections on LinkedIn is a sign of their effective networking activity. This is wrong. It's far better to have 25 network connections that are structured, composed, and engaged with you and that will deliver effectively on your needs and goals. Don't be afraid to decline a request to 'connect' and think about how every new request will add to or dilute your personal brand and core message. Cross and Thomas (2011) argued this point well when saying that you need to think about the composition of your networks by analysing it, delayering it when necessary, and capitalizing on it to produce rewarding and productive relationships.

As for network *engagement* activity, you need to ensure that you engage continuously with your stakeholders, users, and followers. North and Oliver (2104: 3) argued that your audiences 'will expect a continuous delivery of content through digital platforms. You can't just use a digital platform when it suits you.' Once you have given the audiences in your network a taste of what you can deliver as a researcher, they will want more and if you don't provide this on a regular basis, they will quickly desert you for other researchers on other platforms. So, rather than simply placing a conference or peer-reviewed paper on a digital platform and leaving it, you need to think about how you engage with the people that view and download your paper. For example, you could set up a

Google Scholar Alert so that every time one of your papers is cited, you can contact that person and ask for critical feedback, or suggest that they read another related paper that you have had published, or perhaps send them a lecture presentation associated with your paper. Some platforms like Academia. edu allow you get critical feedback on a working paper from within your network. Again, this will help you not only to get feedback, it will also allow you to keep up your communication and engagement levels with people within your networks. You may consider this type of ongoing engagement to be a drain on your time, but it really needs to be considered as an investment in the relationship with the people in your networks. As Ibarra and Hunter (2007: 44) argued in relation to managers, the 'word "work" is part of networking, and it is not easy work, because it involves reaching outside the borders of a manager's comfort zone'. Indeed, this engagement activity will keep the people within your network engaged and interested in your research and it will be you that reaps the benefits of increased citations and the resultant H and I index scores in the long term. Both of these indices are important in terms of demonstrating the citation impact of your work. For example, an H-index score of 10 means that you have 10 published research papers that have been cited at least 10 times. The I-index score, on the other hand, measures the 'contemporary nature' of your research by looking at the number of published papers and their citations, but only in the last 5 years.

It is also worth remembering that this type of ongoing engagement with your audiences helps you to build and develop your online reputation. Indeed, Madden and Smith (2010) found that online reputation management is becoming increasingly important and is evidenced by an increasing number of recruiters scanning a range of digital platforms when assessing the strengths and weaknesses of potential job candidates.

Conclusion

Much of the previous discussion has been framed around the need to think strategically about what you do as a researcher and how you can stand out in the crowd. The digital landscape has undeniably created a vast array of opportunities for researchers to develop their digital profile, access new networks, and extend the reach and impact of their research outputs. The trouble is that these opportunities are available to all researchers, and so the real question is, how do you stand out in a crowded marketplace?

In a world that has gone digital, Ahmed and Olander (2012) concluded that a Smith & Wesson will always beat four aces. What they mean by this is that new digital technologies have changed the nature of the game and the old rules don't apply any more. What was once considered a winning hand now looks ridiculous in the face of a powerful new technology. The digitally agile researcher needs to re-evaluate their previous assumptions about how research is conducted and disseminated and take advantage of the new rules that are shaping the digital landscape.

> ## Best Practice
>
> • The digital world means that you need to recalibrate, plan, set a new direction, and understand the metrics that matter.
> • Develop a distinctive academic profile by identifying a set of values, a core message, and point of differentiation.
> • Build and develop your online reputation with the right networks.
> • Think of networking as a systematic process that focuses on structure, composition, and engagement.

Further reading

Casciaro, T., Gino, F. and Kouchaki, M. (2016) Learn to love networking, *Harvard Business Review*, 94 (5): 104–107.

Ibarra, H. and Hunter, M. (2007) How leaders create and use networks, *Harvard Business Review*, 85 (1): 40–47.

References

Ahmed, A. and Olander, S. (2012) *Velocity: The seven new laws for a world gone digital.* London: Random House.

Byham, W.C. (2009) Start networking right away (even if you hate it), *Harvard Business Review*, 87 (1): 22.

Casciaro, T., Gino, F. and Kouchaki, M. (2016) Learn to love networking, *Harvard Business Review*, 94 (5): 104–107.

Cross, R. and Thomas, R. (2011) A smarter way to network, *Harvard Business Review*, 89 (7/8): 149–153.

Haferkamp, N. and Krämer, N.C. (2011) Social comparison 2.0: examining the effects of online profiles on social-networking sites, *Cyberpsychology, Behavior, and Social Networking*, 14 (5): 309–314.

Hood, K.M., Robles, M. and Hopkins, C.D. (2014) Personal branding and social media for students in today's competitive job market, *Journal of Research in Business Education*, 56 (2): 33.

Ibarra, H. and Hunter, M. (2007) How leaders create and use networks, *Harvard Business Review*, 85 (1): 40–47.

Madden, M. and Smith, A. (2010) *Reputation Management and Social Media.* Washington, DC: Pew Research Center.

North, S. and Oliver, J.J. (2014) A strategic look at how to extend your digital footprint. *Strategic Direction*, 30 (7): 1–3.

Poeppelman, T. and Blacksmith, N. (2014) Personal branding via social media: increasing SIOP visibility one member at a time, *Industrial-Organizational Psychologist*, 51 (3): 112–119.

Uzzi, B. and Dunlap, S. (2005) How to build your network, *Harvard Business Review*, 83 (12): 53–60.

Wetsch, L.R. (2012) A personal branding assignment using social media, *Journal of Advertising Education*, 16 (1): 30.

Planning for engaged research: a collaborative 'Labcast'

Richard Holliman, Gareth Davies,
Victoria Pearson, Trevor Collins,
Simon Sheridan, Helen Brown,
Jenny Hallam and Mark Russell

Introduction

How can you plan effectively for engagement? This chapter offers practical
advice on how to respond to this important question in a pragmatic way. Our
thinking is based on support we have offered to researchers through two related
culture change projects: one designed to embed an engagement strategy and
improve the quality of engaged research at The Open University in the UK
(Holliman et al., 2015); the other to develop a more structured, sustainable, and
aspirational culture for school–university engagement with research (Holliman
and Davies, 2015).

In this chapter, we introduce a framework developed to support researchers
who are planning for public engagement with research. As such, we have written
this account primarily from a researcher perspective, but also with input from
non-academic stakeholders. For the purposes of this chapter, we take non-
academic stakeholders to include end-users, members of the public, and any
other non-academic beneficiaries. Hence, a further aspiration is that a range of
non-academic stakeholders could also adapt the framework to inform their nego-
tiations with researchers. In the context of the activity we discuss in this chapter,
non-academic stakeholders include teachers. It could also have included the
participating students.

In what follows, we offer an authentic worked example of the framework in
action, involving an activity mediated via digital tools and technologies and
involving scientists, an educational technologist, several teachers, 25 sixth-form
students, and an evaluation researcher. It is important to note, therefore, that the

framework is designed to be flexible and adaptable beyond this worked example. We have developed it from our experience of advising Open University academics from across a wide range of disciplines, consultation with Research Councils UK (RCUK) and the National Coordinating Centre for Public Engagement (NCCPE), other projects funded through the School–University Partnership Initiative (SUPI) (RCUK, 2013), and our collaboration with Denbigh Teaching School Alliance. The framework should be applicable to any researcher and discipline, and all forms of engaged research.

A planning framework in six 'Ps'

Given the confusion about definitions of engagement (see, for example, Jensen and Holliman, 2016), we begin our exploration of the planning framework by considering what we mean by engagement. In the context of research, we offer the following definition:

> Engaged research encompasses the different ways that researchers meaning-fully interact with various stakeholders[1] over any or all stages of a research process, from issue formulation, the production or co-creation of new knowledge, to knowledge evaluation and dissemination.
>
> [1]The term stakeholders includes members of the public, end-users, etc., in effect, any non-academic actor that contributes in some way to the research process.
>
> (adapted from Grand et al., 2015: 14)

Why, then, should researchers engage in this way? We argue that there are two main reasons: (1) to improve the quality of research, and (2) to improve the impacts arising from the research for those who participate in its production and those affected by the outcomes (Holliman and Warren, 2017).

Ideally, engaged research should address both reasons. In this chapter, we focus on the second, in particular, in relation to ethical standards. Engaged research should be undertaken based on the understanding that researchers take account of the potential impact it could have on stakeholders. In this context, we refer both to the risk of harm as well as the potential benefit, effect, and/or change it may have on stakeholders. Such an approach requires careful upstream planning (including clearance from institutional ethics committees), downstream project management through the research cycle, and effective forms of governance (for discussion, see Wilsdon and Willis, 2004).

What questions can help to shape upstream planning for engagement? We argue that effective planning should take account of the dimensions of engaged research, which we represent as six 'Ps': preparedness, politics, publics, purposes, processes and performance (adapted from Holliman, 2013). In the following sections, we introduce each of the dimensions in turn as a separate stage in the planning process. It is, however, important to note that the dimensions are interrelated – as you make decisions in relation to one, it could influence one or more other dimensions. It follows that, as the planning for engagement progresses, researchers (and stakeholders involved in the planning) need to reflect back on the earlier decisions to check and revise accordingly.

First step: Preparedness

In reading this chapter, you are already in the process of preparing for engagement. Before you embark further on a path to embed engagement within your research, the next questions you should consider are: why do you want to engage and why might stakeholders want to engage with you? Alternatively, do you see genuine value in engaging research (i.e. intrinsic value) or do you feel you 'have to' engage (i.e. extrinsic value)?

As a first step in preparing to engage, you should look to provide provisional answers to these questions, and to reflect on why you have answered them in the way that you have. For example, you may be working in a university or unit where engagement is seen as second nature. If this is the case, look for an institutional or unit policy for engagement and seek out colleagues who could support and mentor your work. Alternatively, if you cannot identify any stakeholders who may want to work with you, try looking for examples in your field of research. But we also urge caution in selecting your examples. Look for examples that address both challenges and benefits arising from processes of engagement. (The NCCPE Case Studies listed in the cited resources at the end of this chapter are a good place to start.) As with anything else in life, if it looks too good to be true, beware. No engagement activity has ever been planned for, delivered, and received without issues, challenges or problems. Practices can always be improved upon through evidence-based critical reflection.

Alternatively, if you feel that you are only engaging because it is a requirement of a given funder and/or your institution, we urge caution. 'Do no damage' should be the mantra for all research projects. For any project that involves engagement, this includes stakeholders who contribute. As a researcher you have a responsibility to act ethically and in good faith in all research activities (see, for example, DIUS, 2007). Do not enter into the process of engaged research half-heartedly or without relevant expertise within your team, and always seek advice about the ethics of working with stakeholders, for example, by contacting your institution's ethics committee. (The NCCPE-hosted resources, 'Ethics in Community-Based Participatory Research', listed in the cited resources at the end of this chapter might be useful.)

To illustrate the level of preparedness we are advocating, we refer to a digitally mediated 'Labcast' activity, which is an interactive, live web broadcast that integrates video streaming and instant messaging to enable a conversation between two or more locations (Pearson et al., 2016). This activity was organized through an existing school–university partnership called 'Engaging Opportunities'. As such, university researchers were working as a matter of routine with senior

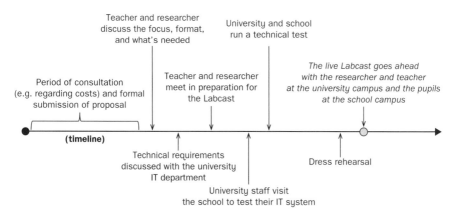

Figure 9.1 Timeline of the events leading up to a Labcast activity carried out with a school in the Milton Keynes area

leaders (e.g. Helen Brown) in local schools, and we had received ethical approval from The Open University to work with children and young people under certain conditions. Our existing partnership allowed us to respond quickly to a funding scheme designed to bring 'cutting-edge research into the classroom'. If you do not have an established school–university partnership to draw on, you should use this preparatory stage to establish relationships with relevant stakeholders (see 'Publics' on p. 92).

Open University researchers worked collaboratively with Denbigh School teachers in Milton Keynes to produce a proposal for the Labcast. The planning of the Labcast is mapped as a continuum (Figure 9.1). The submitted bid covered the costs of hosting an interactive web broadcast from a university research laboratory to a classroom of A-level Physics students (Pearson et al., 2016). In so doing, we paired a physics teacher (Jenny Hallam) with a space science researcher (Simon Sheridan), as the latter was involved in the development of one of the scientific instruments on board the recent Rosetta mission to explore a comet (67P/Churyumov-Gerasimenko) that is travelling through our solar system (Wright et al., 2015).

Second step: Politics

The politics of engaged research, not least in the context of school–university engagement, are many and varied. In a chapter of this length, and with a focus on practical advice, we can only scratch the surface. However, an understanding of the political context of your engagement is crucial. In the not-so-distant past, questions about engaged research would almost certainly not have been a consideration for many researchers. This changed, in the UK at least, with the introduction of the impact agenda, which, in effect, introduced a requirement to generate evidence of the social and/or economic impacts from research (RCUK, 2010).

Many funding bodies now require the submission of an 'acceptable' pathways-to-impact plan, or equivalent, before research can begin. Furthermore, in the context of school–university engagement, universities will have their own strategic priorities, for example, efforts to widen participation in higher education. In addition, audits of research, such as the Research Excellence Framework (REF), have a role in assessing the quality of research alongside the impacts this work generates throughout the cycle of research (DBEIS, 2016).

It follows that impacts should not be something you only anticipate materializing at the end of the process and your focus should not be limited to those who have conventionally engaged with the outputs of your research. Instead, you should be taking full advantage of the opportunities to engage relevant stakeholders with the research process – making sure plans are in place to evaluate the impact this has on researchers, stakeholders, and the research, so you can demonstrate the return on investment offered to funders.

In the case of the Labcast, we had the remit of 'bringing cutting-edge science into the classroom' through a professional development programme for teachers (RCUK, 2014). As such, teachers were key participants in our engagement, as were school students. As we organized the activity to be delivered within the school timetable, these participants were influenced by the requirements of the National Curriculum and the audit conditions of the Office for Standards in Education, Children's Services and Skills (Ofsted). (Notably, many school–university engagement activities are organized as extracurricular activities, which are considered under the audit conditions of Ofsted.) In contrast, the researchers were engaging within the political context of the research impact agenda and the potential audit conditions of the REF. It follows that the identification of (complementary) reasons to engage is an important aspect of the politics of engagement (see 'Purposes' on p. 94).

Third step: Publics

This stage requires an understanding of which parties have a stake in research, and of these, who you will endeavour to engage. In our experience, while defining publics for your engaged research may seem obvious, it is fraught with challenges, not least in agreeing who is and is not a public. We have encountered many examples of researchers defining 'the public' as a single entity; to paraphrase, 'It is my intention to engage the wider public with my research.' In other instances, researchers have ruled out working beyond established groups. In our experience, these are not helpful places to start. Rather, we suggest that researchers explore who the 'publics in particular' could be for a given engaged research endeavour (Michael, 2009). This more specific articulation of 'publics' allows the researcher to consider smaller, identifiable stakeholders and groups, and to tailor the purposes and processes of activities to ensure they are relevant and meaningful to those participating.

Our solution to the challenges of defining 'publics', which was also informed by research (Grand et al., 2015; Jensen and Holliman, 2016) and by the work of

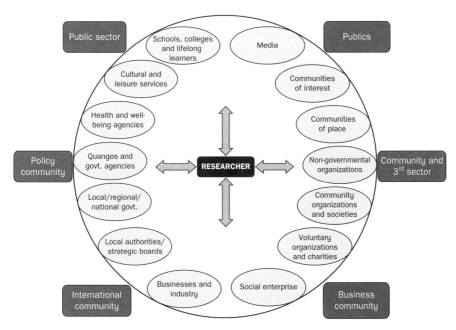

Figure 9.2 Mapping the different external groups with whom researchers might engage

Source: NCCPE [https://www.publicengagement.ac.uk].

the National Coordinating Centre for Public Engagement (NCCPE; Figure 9.2), is therefore to think more broadly about non-academic stakeholders, but then to narrow this list down to those who could usefully add value in terms of knowledge production and/or those affected by the outcomes. (These may or may not be the same people.)

Anyone who is not employed by a university has the potential to be a non-academic stakeholder. Hence, ask yourself which stakeholders are you already working with, who else do you want to work with, and who wants to contribute? Furthermore, are there stakeholders whom you would not want to engage with and why? It is also important to note at this point that a given stakeholder does not necessarily have to commit to all stages of the research cycle. As we have argued elsewhere:

> Engaged research requires different forms of expertise, whose relevance will wax and wane depending on the research and on the point in the research cycle where engagement happens.
>
> (Grand et al., 2015: 3)

In the case of the Engaging Opportunities partnership, our key stakeholders were children and young people, aged 11–19, studying in schools and further education colleges in Milton Keynes. We also agreed to work with teachers from these schools, and with Senior Leaders within the Denbigh Teaching School

Alliance. To this end, we ensured that funding was made available through the project to support the work of a schools-based Project Coordinator (Mark Russell). Mark supported Helen Brown (a senior teacher) who set up the Labcast, liaising with teachers and pupils at the school and Open University researchers (predominantly Victoria Pearson and Trevor Collins). The Project Coordinator also helped to recruit the pupils and teacher for this activity.

Fourth step: Purposes

Having consolidated information from the first three steps ('Preparedness', 'Politics', and 'Publics'), you will have an understanding: (1) of the wider context for engaged research; (2) how the proposed activity is characterized by political issues at the societal, institutional, and stakeholder levels; and (3) who the participants are, or could be, for a given collaborative endeavour. The next stage entails purposes: what are the aims and objectives of the engaged research, and if funding is being sought, how do they meet the requirements of the funder?

The Engaging Opportunities project had the following aims, which were agreed by the key stakeholders on the project before we submitted our proposal to the funder (RCUK):

* To inspire young people aged 11–19 from schools and further education colleges in Milton Keynes, providing role models to aspire to.
* To develop activities that help to build confidence and self-efficacy among students from a diversity of backgrounds and abilities.
* To generate awareness of the nature and challenges of contemporary research.
* To support those who wish to make the transition from school to university, while facilitating discussion about the social, economic, and ethical impacts of research, developing the skills and competencies necessary to become effective citizens.

Ideally, the purposes (which could take the form of aims or objectives) should also be discussed and agreed 'upstream' with the stakeholders (i.e. in advance of submitting a research proposal). At the very least, the aims and objectives of your activity will need to be shared with your stakeholders before they agree to participate. This could take the form of an official letter inviting participation. One of the reasons for this is to support the principles of informed consent (Miller and Bell, 2002). It is also an exercise in managing expectations, ensuring that you do not create unrealistic expectations about what can be achieved. It follows that the objectives of the activity need to be clearly agreed by all involved, making sure you have made provision so that the research is carried out according to the criteria laid out in your ethics review ('Preparedness') and reflected in the type(s) of knowledge, data, methods of data collection, and techniques of analysis you will use to evaluate the potential impacts of the engaged research ('Performance').

Having agreed a set of aims, you need to decide on the specific objectives, with a view to using them to inform evidence collection and/or evaluation of performance. It follows that your objectives need to be Specific, Measurable, Achievable, Relevant, and Time-bound (SMART), and be supported by relevant Key Performance Indicators (KPIs) and/or metrics. The objectives of the Labcast, for example, were:

- To provide students with access to an authentic research laboratory without taking them out of school.
- To engage students with cutting-edge research via the Key Stage 4 curriculum.
- To provide an effective professional development activity for teachers and researchers.

Fifth step: Processes

Exploring processes is all about how, when, where, and through what media the engagement will take place. In other words, what are the methodologies and methods of the engaged research? How will the research involve relevant stakeholders in meaningful ways? When, and how often, will stakeholders be involved in the research cycle? Where are these interventions likely to take place, and through what mechanisms? And have the processes been discussed with the stakeholders to ensure they work for them?

One of the main challenges in planning for the processes of engagement is the sheer number of possible options for conducting activities. In exploring these issues in the past, we have found it useful to begin this process by considering a methodological framework devised by Irwin (2008) (see Table 9.1).

Irwin (2008) describes three orders of engagement – first, second, and third – as, in effect, ideal types. Each order has characteristics that lend themselves to particular methods of engagement. As an example, first-order engagement is mainly about communication. This could be useful towards the end of the research when there are findings to be publicized. Second-order engagement lends itself to dialogue, which could be useful when consulting with a particular stakeholder on the direction of research. Finally, third-order engagement involves multiple stakeholders, which could be useful in the planning phase, and in connecting the findings of a complex engaged research project to the development of public policy and/or practice.

In our experience, both as active researchers applying for funds but also as peers supporting and reviewing potential applications, we have seen that some researchers have approached grant preparation with trepidation, given the requirements around pathways to impact. They can be risk-averse, not wanting to introduce anything into a grant application that might reduce their chances of being funded in what is a very competitive process. In effect, this can stifle creativity and lead to bland forms of engagement that fail to do justice to the needs of stakeholders (Holliman and Jensen, 2009). Our advice is to combine 'tried-and-tested' methods with at least one activity that is new to either the researchers and/or the participating stakeholders.

Table 9.1 Characteristics of first-, second-, and third-order thinking

	First-order	Second-order	Third-order
Main focus	Public ignorance and technical education	Dialogue, engagement, transparency, building trust	Direction, quality and need for socio-technical change
Key issues	Communicating science, informing debate, getting the facts straight	Re-establishing public confidence, building consensus, encouraging debate, addressing uncertainty	Setting science and technology in wider cultural context, enhancing reflexivity and critical analysis
Communication style	One-way, top-down	Two-way, bottom-up	Multiple stakeholders, multiple frameworks
Model of scientific governance	Science-led, 'science' and 'politics' kept apart	Transparency, responsive to public opinion, accountable	Open to contested problem definitions, beyond government alone, addressing societal concerns and priorities
Socio-technical challenge	Maintaining rationality, encouraging scientific progress and expert independence	Establishing broad societal consensus	Viewing heterogeneity, conditionality, and disagreement as a societal resource
Overall perspective	Focusing on science	Focusing on communication and engagement	Focusing on scientific/political cultures

Source: Irwin (2008: 208).

A further solution to this challenge is to plan upstream with stakeholders, which is what we did with the Labcast. We initially selected this method because: (1) it provided access to a working laboratory and busy researcher; (2) it allowed more opportunities for curriculum links than a 'lab tour' format; (3) it did not require students to be taken off timetable or transport costs to be found; (4) it had fewer implications for laboratories that are heavily used; and (5) it contextualized researchers and their science in an authentic working environment.

We used the Labcast format to deliver a physics lesson, from a laboratory at the Open University's Walton Hall Campus (Figure 9.3), to an A-level class of 25 students based at Denbigh School in Milton Keynes (Figure 9.4).

Figure 9.3   Simon Sheridan and Jenny Hallam delivering the 'Labcast' at The Open University, facilitated by the technical team

Photo: Victoria Pearson.

Figure 9.4   The 'Labcast' activity in action, Denbigh School, Milton Keynes

Photo: Mark Russell.

Figure 9.5   The technical team mixing the live stream and other content

Photo: Victoria Pearson.

The Labcast incorporated:

- first-order engagement, for example, presenting to camera, interviews (featuring Jenny Hallam and Simon Sheridan), and the use of third-party videos (from ESA and NASA);
- second-order interactive elements, in the form of a Q&A session, a maths workshop, and a lab experiment mirrored in the laboratory and the school.

As we have noted, authenticity was a key consideration for this activity. The researcher (Simon Sheridan) is a Rosetta Mission scientist involved in the design and build of the OU's Ptolemy instrument on board the European Space Agency's *Philae lander*. He was, at the time of the Labcast, engaged in interpretation of data from the comet's surface (Wright et al., 2015). Furthermore, the Labcast format gave us access to the laboratory used for testing the Ptolemy ground reference model.

The Labcast was recorded and mixed in real-time by three audio-visual experts (Figure 9.5). The team used static and roving cameras, 'webcasting' as a high-definition video stream via FaceTime™.

Sixth step: Performance

Researchers have found that one of the key challenges in engaged research is the assessment of performance (Grand et al., 2015; Watermeyer, 2016). We argue that addressing a lack of routine evaluation could help raise quality in engaged research. Publication of evaluation studies would result in an evidence base, effectively shared, demonstrating track records and critically reflective practitioners. From this evidence base, measures of excellence could be identified, with researchers and stakeholders being recognized and rewarded for excellent work. In turn, this would help to improve cultures of engaged research, demonstrating to researchers the aspirational nature of progressive approaches to engaged research.

It follows that this sixth and final dimension of engaged research is crucial to improving practice. To start this process, you should remind yourself of why and how you plan to assess performance. This requires that you keep your focus on your SMART objectives ('Purposes'), while also remaining open enough to report on unexpected developments, outcomes, and/or impacts. It also requires that you have considered the resources you need to evaluate and, if relevant, collect evidence of research impact. Do you have the resources within the existing research team to conduct an assessment of performance? Have you allocated resources for career development if this is required? Alternatively, have you included funding to employ an independent evaluator?

For the Labcast activity we collected evidence of performance from the pupils, teacher, and researcher. Our goals were to evaluate the challenges and impacts of giving students an authentic experience of engaging with a research scientist in their laboratory; providing the opportunity to engage with cutting-edge science within the curriculum; and providing development opportunities for teachers and researchers.

In total, there were seven Open University staff (including a project coordinator, technical staff, and a research scientist), five teachers (an early career physics teacher in the Open University laboratory, and a senior leader, the Project Coordinator, and two teachers supported at the school), and 25 students (all of whom were in Year 12 studying A-level Physics at the time of the Labcast). For the purposes of evaluation, we chose to focus our efforts on gathering insights from the physics teacher, the research scientist, and the students. Figure 9.6, an updated version of Figure 9.1, summarizes our evaluation strategy, identifying pre- and post-Labcast measures of the teacher's, researcher's, and students' experiences.

The Labcast was designed to offer students an authentic experience of research by engaging them via a webcast with a professional scientist from a research laboratory in the university. Many authors advocate the importance of giving children and young people authentic experiences of science by engaging them in real-life issues, where theory is put into practice (Monroe, 2003; Ballantyne and Packer, 2009). For example, studies have shown that teachers providing more authentic opportunities in science have resulted in students having a stronger comprehension (Purcell-Gates et al., 2007).

The format of the Labcast was designed to promote authenticity by demonstrating how equations taught at A-level Physics had been used to calculate the landing of the *Philae lander* on a comet (67P/Churyumov-Gerasimenko), hence bridging the divide between theory and practice. By carrying out pre- and post-interviews with the physics teacher we learnt that, from her perspective, the Labcast had met the key objectives. It helped the pupils move beyond the 'very theoretical' to the more practical and tangible understanding of 'a real-life research situation'. She explained that a conventional lesson can fail to get students to 'think about the wider picture'', but said that the Labcast was an

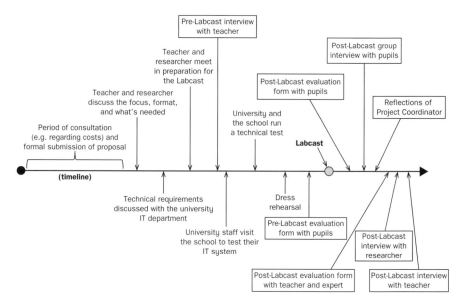

Figure 9.6   Timeline of the evaluation activities (in boxes), mapped against the Labcast activity

effective mechanism for 'inspiring students and also demonstrating subject knowledge as well, good subject knowledge'.

From pre- and post-Labcast evaluation forms and a post-Labcast group interview with the students, we learnt that from their perspective the Labcast had also met the key objectives: 'The amount we learnt in the Labcast I would say would normally take us about three lessons'; 'It's more enjoyable [than a lesson], something that helped stick in the brain.' Moreover, the teacher explained that the students benefited by getting 'to see behind the scenes [. . .] [and] some of the real difficulties which are in planning an actual science mission'.

The teacher explained that the students also got to experience a 'lightbulb moment' when they understood that the researcher was 'just like anyone else', and it increased the students' awareness of the large timeframes and costs characterizing contemporary research. We learnt that for some students, this changed their perspectives of a researcher's role from that of 'drinking coffee and talking' to 'demanding but rewarding'. It provided students with 'a more in-depth knowledge of how research works', boosting some of the students' confidence in their ability to succeed in a research career. Yet for others, it changed the off-putting factors of being a researcher from 'boring' and 'underpaid' to 'amount of qualifications', 'deadlines', and 'dedication to specific field'.

The Labcast was designed to engage the participants with cutting-edge science. One of the objectives was to give the teacher opportunities to update her knowledge of her subject, empowering her to encourage students to explore scientific developments and associated social issues. This resulted in students understanding the opportunities available to them. 'I didn't really know there were so many different aspects that you could actually go into in a project like that.' For others, it helped them to understand the role they could play in science:

> For me, I always wanted to pursue a career in engineering. I thought that engin-eering was kind of sectioned off from the science till I saw how they were talking about how engineers were saying different things to them [. . .] it's opened another door for me or another options which I could take.

The planning and hosting of the Labcast were intended to provide development opportunities for the teacher and researcher. From the teacher's perspective, we learnt that this was achieved in the planning stage by demonstrating the ability to incorporate factors such as 'action learning' into the lesson plan. Having taken part in the Labcast, the teacher said the experience of engaging with the contem-porary research and researcher was valuable in itself because it had given them ideas of how they might improve their style of teaching: 'I think I am going to try and link more up-to-date research and discoveries into topics that I teach if they are suitable so that the students are aware of areas which are current because I think that's part of what engaged them.'

In a post-Labcast interview with the researcher, we learnt that, from their perspective, the Labcast offered valuable development opportunities for a research career because of how it 'hinge[s] on being able to [. . .] get compli-cated ideas and concepts across [. . .] to people who may have never seen these things or heard of these things before'. In particular, we learnt that the planning stage offered the opportunity to learn about teaching in a school context: 'I think it's ways of trying to tie into the curriculum stuff that's happening out in the big wide world.'

Evaluation should inform critical reflection and changes in practice. From the evaluation, we learnt a number of lessons to consider before planning future Labcasts. The planning phase was crucial. The teacher and researcher went through a process of having to redefine their preconceived ideas of what role they would play and what they hoped to gain from their experience. We also learnt that the students didn't really know what to expect. Better information prior to the Labcast could help with this in future. Pragmatically, we experienced a tension between quality and informality and authenticity, as in deciding to have a 'messy' laboratory versus a studio set-up.

Summary

Engaged research is more labour-intensive and can feel more challenging than carrying out research in a disciplinary vacuum. In part, this is simply because the number of expert voices with a stake in the research increases. Although we are clearly advocating engaged research as a way of making its processes and products more meaningful and relevant to a wider group of stakeholders, it is essential that you do not underestimate the challenges of working outside your discipline and/or professional area of expertise. Furthermore, you should take account of the time it can take to find engaging opportunities that have a realistic chance of delivering your and your stakeholders' desired impacts (noting that not all stakeholders will agree on all of the desired impacts).

The time and skills required to evaluate impacts can also be underestimated, increasing the likelihood you will not be able to demonstrate, for example, through publication, that you have delivered on what you promised. In turn, this could damage your or your institution's reputation. To avoid this, you should take advantage of the growing body of knowledge in this area (see suggestions at the end of the chapter), and ensure that plans for engaged research are based on the full economic costs of planning for, enacting and collating evidence of the impacts. (This does not mean that a funder will necessarily pay the full economic costs. Rather, participants should fully cost the plans and agree the level of resource commitment with the respective institutions, employers, etc., through whatever means are possible. This may require your institution, employer, etc., to underwrite some of the costs to ensure you have time to complete the tasks effectively.)

To illustrate the point, Figure 9.7 demonstrates one way of accounting for the amount of time each stakeholder needs to contribute to an engaged research activity (for discussion, see Holliman and Davies, 2015). And Figure 9.8 illustrates the commitment of time required by the pupils, teachers, and university staff to participate in the Labcast.

Finally, it is important to recognize that the strategic benefits of engaging stakeholders can far outweigh the time and effort invested. Responding proactively and collaboratively to the principles of engaged research can improve your work and diversify your skills. Done excellently, it will enhance your career as you: (1) develop a track record of evidence-based critical reflection; (2) generate funding from external sources; and (3) publish outputs, for example, in peer-reviewed academic journals, but also evidenced through other 'legacies'

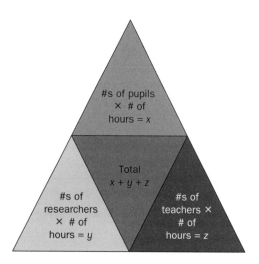

Figure 9.7 The formula for the SUPI metric

Source: Holliman and Davies (2015).

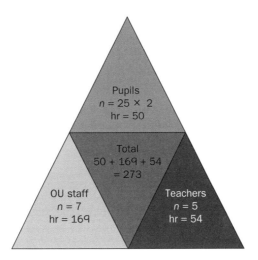

Figure 9.8 The SUPI metric calculation for the Labcast activity

(e.g. Pearson et al., 2016). With this in mind, we note that UK universities are becoming more aware of the need to create the conditions where excellence in engaged research can flourish (Holliman et al., 2015). Acknowledging that significant challenges remain in this area (TNS BMRB, 2015; Watermeyer, 2016), we also note the increasing number of UK universities that now include pathways for researchers to evidence excellence in engaged research in promotion cases (Holliman, 2015). This embeds a culture that gives researchers confidence to collaborate with stakeholders as they plan upstream, manage their collective projects downstream, and share the evidence of the social and economic impacts of their shared labours.

Common Pitfalls

- Leaving planning for engaged research too late – begin your planning upstream, ideally with relevant stakeholders, and work collaboratively downstream.
- Not fully costing/justifying resources – be realistic about the full economic costs of engaged research and seek assurances from stakeholders that they have the resources they need to participate.

Best Practice

- Write an elevator pitch about your research and 'road test' this with your key stakeholders. Are the objectives of your research clear, and do they have the potential to match or complement at least some of the aims of your stakeholders?

- Plan for more than one type of social or economic impact, combining methodologies that you have tried and tested in the past with at least one imaginative and bold initiative that is new to you and/or your stakeholders.
- Think through the potential risks of your planned activities and revise accordingly; assess ethical implications and seek advice and institutional approval to ensure no harm is done.
- Talk early and talk often with your stakeholders, including plans for how the various participants would like to be acknowledged/attributed in any outputs from the work.

Cited resources

Designing public-centric forms of public engagement with research [http://www.open.ac.uk/blogs/per/?page_id=6194]
Ethics in Community-Based Participatory Research [https://www.publicengagement.ac.uk/work-with-us/current-projects/ethics-cbpr]
NCCPE Case Studies [https://www.publicengagement.ac.uk/case-studies]
The digital attributes of engaged researchers [http://weblab.open.ac.uk/dper]

Acknowledgements

Several of the ideas, workshop activities, and tools discussed in this chapter were funded through an award made as part of the RCUK School–University Partnership Initiative [EP/K027786/1; http://www.rcuk.ac.uk/pe/PartnershipsInitiative] and a further award made through the RCUK Public Engagement with Research Catalysts [EP/J020087/1; http://www.rcuk.ac.uk/pe/embedding]. The Labcast was funded through an RCUK 'Bringing Cutting-Edge Science into the Classroom' Award [https://www.stem.org.uk/cpd-partners]. We acknowledge the many contributors to these projects, and to the Labcast activity in particular, notably: Andrew Squires (Denbigh School); Kate Bradshaw, Nicholas Braithwaite, Diane Ford, Ben Hawkridge, and Chris Valentine (The Open University); Claire Wood (NCCPE); and Jenni Chambers (RCUK). Jane Perrone provided helpful comments on a draft of this chapter. Finally, we acknowledge the contributions of the students who participated in the Labcast.

References

Ballantyne, R. and Packer, J. (2009) Introducing a fifth pedagogy: experience-based strategies for facilitating learning in natural environments, *Environmental Education Research*, 15 (2): 243–262 [retrieved from: https://espace.library.uq.edu.au/view/UQ:195346/UQ195346_postprint.pdf; accessed 5 August 2016].
Department for Innovation, Universities and Skills (DIUS) (2007) *Rigour, Respect and Responsibility: A universal ethical code for scientists*. London: DIUS [retrieved

from: https://www.gov.uk/government/uploads/system/uploads/attachment_data/file/283157/universal-ethical-code-scientists.pdf; accessed 5 August 2016].

Department of Business, Energy and Industrial Strategy (2016) *Building on Success and Learning from Experience: An independent review of the Research Excellence Framework*. London: HMSO [retrieved from: https://www.gov.uk/government/uploads/system/uploads/attachment_data/file/541338/ind-16-9-ref-stern-review.pdf; accessed 3 August 2016].

Grand, A., Davies, G., Holliman, R. and Adams, A. (2015) Mapping public engagement with research in a UK university, *PLoS ONE*, 10 (4): 1–19 [retrieved from: http://oro.open.ac.uk/43126; accessed 5 August 2016].

Holliman, R. (2013) An engaging thesis, *National Coordinating Centre for Public Engagement Blog*, 7 October [retrieved from: https://www.publicengagement.ac.uk/blog/engaging-thesis; accessed 10 May 2016].

Holliman, R. (2015) Valuing engaged research, *Euroscientist Webzine*, 4 November [retrieved from: http://www.euroscientist.com/valuing-publicly-engaged-research; accessed 10 May 2016].

Holliman, R., Adams, A., Blackman, T., Collins, T., Davies, G., Dibb, S. et al. (2015) *An Open Research University: Final report*. Milton Keynes: The Open University [retrieved from: http://oro.open.ac.uk/44255; accessed 10 May 2016].

Holliman, R. and Davies, G. (2015) Moving beyond the seductive siren of reach: planning for the social and economic impacts emerging from school–university engagement with research, *Journal of Science Communication*, 14(03), C06, 1–10 [retrieved from: http://oro.open.ac.uk/44415; accessed 10 May 2016].

Holliman, R. and Jensen, E. (2009) (In)authentic science and (im)partial publics: (re)constructing the science outreach and public engagement agenda, in R. Holliman, E. Whitelegg, E. Scanlon, S. Smidt and J. Thomas (eds) *Investigating Science Communication in the Information Age: Implications for public engagement and popular media* (pp. 35–52). Oxford: Oxford University Press.

Holliman, R. and Warren, C.J. (2017) Supporting future scholars of engaged research, *Research for All*, 1 (1): 168–184 [retrieved from: http://www.ingentaconnect.com/contentone/ioep/rfa/2017/00000001/00000001/art00014].

Irwin, A. (2008) Risk, science and public communication: third-order thinking about scientific culture, in M. Bucchi and B. Trench (eds) *Public Communication of Science and Technology Handbook* (pp. 199–212). London: Routledge.

Jensen, E. and Holliman, R. (2016) Norms and values in UK science engagement practice, *International Journal of Science Education, Part B: Communication and Public Engagement*, 6 (1): 68–88 [retrieved from: http://oro.open.ac.uk/41889; accessed 10 May 2016].

Michael, M. (2009) Publics performing publics: of PiGs, PiPs and politics, *Public Understanding of Science*, 18 (5): 617–631.

Miller, T. and Bell, L. (2002) Consenting to what? Issues of access, gatekeeping and 'informed' consent, in M. Mauthner, M. Birch and T. Miller (eds) *Ethics in Qualitative Research* (pp. 53–79). London: Sage.

Monroe, M. (2003) Two avenues for encouraging conservation behaviours, *Human Ecology Review*, 10 (2): 113–125 [retrieved from: http://www.humanecologyreview.org/pastissues/her102/102monroe.pdf; accessed 5 June 2016].

Pearson, V., Sheridan, S., Hallam, J., Collins, T., Davies, G., Brown, H. et al. (2016) Labcasts: bringing cutting-edge science to the classroom, *The Engaging Research Blog* [retrieved from: http://www.open.ac.uk/blogs/per/?p=6789; accessed 2 August 2016].

Purcell-Gates, V., Duke, N. and Martineau, J. (2007) Learning to read and write genre-specific texts: roles of authentic experience and explicit teaching, *Reading Research*

Quarterly, 42 (1): 8–45 [retrieved from: http://onlinelibrary.wiley.com/doi/10.1598/RRQ.42.1.1/epdf; accessed 5 June 2016].

Research Councils UK (RCUK) (2010) *Concordat for engaging the public with research.* Swindon: RCUK [retrieved from: http://www.rcuk.ac.uk/per/Pages/Concordat.aspx; accessed 10 May 2016].

Research Councils UK (RCUK) (2013) *School–University Partnerships Initiative.* Swindon: RCUK [retrieved from: http://www.rcuk.ac.uk/pe/PartnershipsInitiative; accessed 13 April 2016].

Research Councils UK (RCUK) (2014) *Opportunities for researchers.* Swindon: RCUK [retrieved from: http://www.rcuk.ac.uk/pe/researchers; accessed 3 August 2016].

TNS BMRB (2015) *Factors affecting public engagement by researchers: A study on behalf of a consortium of UK public research funders.* London: Wellcome Trust [retrieved from: http://www.wellcome.ac.uk/stellent/groups/corporatesite/@msh_grants/documents/web_document/wtp060033.pdf; accessed 10 May 2016].

Watermeyer, R. (2016) Public intellectuals vs. new public management: the defeat of public engagement in higher education, *Studies in Higher Education*, 41 (12): 2271–2285 [retrieved from: http://www.tandfonline.com/doi/full/10.1080/03075079.2015.1034261].

Wilsdon, J. and Willis, R. (2004) *See through science: why public engagement needs to move upstream.* London: DEMOS [retrieved from http://www.demos.co.uk/files/Seethroughsciencefinal.pdf?1240939425; accessed 10 May 2016].

Wright, I., Sheridan, S., Barber, S., Morgan, G., Andrews, D. and Morse, A. (2015) CHO-bearing organic compounds at the surface of 67P/Churyumov-Gerasimenko revealed by Ptolemy, *Science*, 349 (6247): aab0673 [retrieved from: http://science.sciencemag.org/content/349/6247/aab0673].

Audio-visual tools for boosting research influence

Christian Payne

Introduction

There is a wealth of multimedia at your fingertips. In addition to posting text on social media sites such as Facebook and Twitter, there are other ways for researchers to engage in online research dialogues and ensure wider impact. This chapter presents ways in which researchers can disseminate short excerpts of work-related information to a wider audience. Examples of using video and audio streams, tips for sharing content and for researching websites are provided, along with proven strategies researchers can implement to signal expertise in a certain domain. Such multimedia blogging or open access publishing can help researchers to share and clarify ideas, build their reputation, and grow their network.

Creating and publishing video and audio data have been greatly facilitated by mobile multimedia technologies and today are easier than ever before. Video production is no longer about shoulder-mounted cameras and editing suites. It has become commonplace to shoot, edit, and upload videos from a smartphone, even for major news organizations. Similarly, for audio content, mobile devices make excellent field recorders enabling the user to capture high-resolution audio in places where lifting a camera might be frowned upon.

Tips and strategies for self-produced video content

The following are some practical suggestions for producing your own video content. The main thing to remember is that video is not complicated. Think of it as many photos accompanied by audio.

Choosing the right video equipment

With so many apps offering easy capture and upload options, you may find all you need to shoot great video is a decent mobile device. I'm happy to shoot, edit, and upload using a phone. On occasion, I may use a larger camera system, or a small weatherproof device should I need to record outside in all weathers. For some videos, there are a few lightweight accessories that can come in handy. As the kit I use tends to evolve on a regular basis, I look for add-ons that not only improve on what my phone can currently do, but that are also compact and portable.

The more equipment we attach to our mobile devices, the closer we get to turning our phones into purpose-made video-capture devices. We also have to remember to carry all those leads and add-ons. If you do find you are shooting a lot of video, then a Wifi-enabled video camera may be a sensible investment, as shooting video can quickly drain a phone's battery.

For ease and simplicity, let us focus on creating video with your existing mobile device. You may already have a smartphone or tablet that is capable of capturing audio and video. With the largest selection of apps designed for multimedia creation, many documentarians, mobile journalists, and film-makers have made the iPhone and iPad their first choice. This is not to say that other devices cannot capture multimedia well. It just means that the majority of apps, microphones, and other add-ons are being designed for Apple devices.

Video quality

People are more likely to engage with your video if it is stable (i.e. not shaky) with clear audio. Good light, a well-framed image, and clear sound will go a long way to help your video reach an audience.

To achieve stable video, you need to keep the camera steady. Feet shoulder-width apart, elbows in. Avoid any sudden pans of movement unless that's the effect you are going for. To prevent 'shaky-cam', you may also find the need for some kind of image stabilization. Some devices have stabilization optically built into the lens. For others, stabilization is enabled by the software. In addition, a pocket tripod can be placed on a desk when filming yourself or others for an extended period of time. The clamps used to hold the phone onto the tripod can vary from device to device but are inexpensive and easy to use.

Pay attention to the sound. It can be more important than the visuals. Bad sound makes a bad video, good sound also makes a podcast. For clear audio, you might need an external microphone (mic). On some smartphones the video mic can be hard to protect from the wind, as it is so close to the lens. In particularly windy conditions, an external mic can make all the difference. The lavalier (lav) or clip-on mic is one I often use. It needs to have the correct connector for your smartphone (either lightning connector or TRRS jack plug for an iPhone). Some Android phones can take either TRS- or TRRS-connected lav mics but it's worth double-checking. An external mic can increase the volume of a person speaking without needing them to get too close to the lens. It can also isolate their voice from background noise and protect from wind distortion.

Make sure you have all the light you need. Natural, diffused light (like you see on an overcast day) looks much better than artificial light or the harsh light of a bright sun. As a rule, keep the light behind you but don't cast a shadow on your subject. Put simply, think of it as 'back to the window, bum to the sun'.

Style

Media organizations, like *The Guardian*, are adopting video policies where two types of production are accepted: 'short, rough and real' or 'polished and professional'. It is almost expected that a live-stream can be 'rough and real'. It could be you are spontaneously filming something unfolding before you. The same applies to short, social video you are sharing to highlight a point. This could be a quick 'how-to' or snatched statement to camera. In contrast, an in-depth report or documentary benefits from more thought in relation to structure and composition. Steady, high-resolution footage will scale well for a variety of screens.

When thinking about style, bear in mind the medium and the platform. Think about your passion and excitement when presenting a subject. Your excitement can be contagious, which is a great vehicle for the information you wish to impart.

Length

The internet is a busy place, so generally speaking, your video shouldn't be too long. The appropriate length will depend on the platform and your audience, but try to say what you can in the most efficient way possible. On YouTube the top ten most popular videos may range in length from 40 seconds to around 9 minutes, with the average video running at about 4 minutes and 20 seconds. YouTube's own search tool will differentiate video length, marking anything 4 minutes or less as 'short' and videos over 20 minutes as 'long'. YouTube allows users to upload a maximum of 15 minutes, unless you have a verified account. Twitter limits all video uploads to 140 seconds unless you are a recognized media producer.

Live-streamed video can and should be longer. Both YouTube and Facebook recognize what is called the 'Golden Window'. This is a key window of time from about 7 to 11 minutes where the real-time viewer has started to interact and share your video with others. It's not unusual to see live-streamed videos that are over 45 minutes long. As questions are asked and comments or icons of appreciation fill the screen, the interaction can be addictive. Sometimes videos will only end with the sudden loss of battery power.

Battery

Make sure you have all the power you will need. Fully charge your device to always be ready and carry extra batteries and a cable to keep it topped up. You might need an external battery or battery case. Shooting, editing, and uploading are heavy on the device's processor power. I carry a couple of options, with a large lead so I can keep the power supply in my pocket and continue to film unhindered. Portable batteries are easy to come by and are widely available online. I choose at least 10,000 mAh in capacity with one or two USB outputs. Check the reviews for the best value and user experience.

Microphones

If you cannot get an inbuilt microphone close to the sound source, you will need some kind of external mic. The kind of mic you use may be dependent on the type of connector your phone has (i.e. minijack, lightning or USB-C). On some occasions, it might be necessary to record the audio separately.

A large selection of microphones is available for mobile devices. Lav mics are the small clip-on microphones you often see at conferences. These are great for one person talking to camera. Two of these microphones can be plugged into a single minijack with the help of a splitter. This can also plug into a lightning adapter for some of the latest devices.

Some microphones like the Shure MV88 will plug directly into the lightning port of your iOS device. No need for cables. However, you will still need to get close to the sound source. All these mics should come with a windshield, or 'spoffle', a small foam cover that protects captured sound from distortion caused by the wind or breath. Even just placing a cheap microphone shield (the type you find covering most mics over the end of your phone) can greatly improve sound quality.

Handheld, wired microphones offer great quality using the lightning connector on iOS devices. The Apogee Mic 96k is not a cheap bit of technology but I've met a few academics who swear by it.

Selfie sticks

As more news agencies cut costs and adopt the practices of the 'video blogger', you too might decide to film yourself as well as your own content. To capture video while interviewing on the move, the 'selfie stick' has taken the place of the second camera operator. These devices – lightweight, extendable poles that you attach your camera to – can take some getting used to. Check the viewing angle of lens on your current device before investing in any of these tools. On most occasions, your arm will be long enough for you to do a piece to camera. If you are looking to walk along with one other person, filming and talking, a selfie stick can come in handy. It will enable you to get a moving wide shot and give the impression that there is a third person doing the camera work. It's possible to hold the selfie stick in one hand and a wired mic in the other. You could also plug two clip-on lav mics into the phone via a splitter. Selfie sticks are hard to hold steady in the wind and in crowded areas an extended selfie stick can be a danger to others. When you have no need to move, a small lightweight tripod is a simpler option.

Video capture apps

The standard on-board video capture app on your device will suffice as you find your feet, but as you gain more confidence in your filming, you will find you crave more control and features. One app being adopted by the film industry and professionals is Filmic Pro, a fully featured video capture app that will give you more control over your focusing, aperture, and sound levels. Professional apps like this can show you real-time audio levels and enable you to set your exposure and focus independently. It will also allow you to record at higher resolutions and file sizes, squeezing the maximum quality available from your device.

Using music in video projects

There may be times when you need some background music for your video projects. The music you select can shape the viewers' emotions around your content. Websites like Marmoset Music [https://www.marmosetmusic.com] and Tune Fruit [https://www.tunefruit.com] have emotional meta-tags, enabling you to choose the right track based on a defined set of parameters.

I also have a playlist on my computer entitled 'Free To Use'. These are songs and tracks I have written or that were made by friends. Some are available through certain licensing that means I can use the music in my videos providing I credit the creator.

What makes an engaging video?

A good story

Quality is an abstract concept and the result of perception. The quality perceived by the viewer will be based on how much value they receive from it. Is it easy to follow, useful, and enlightening? Is it interesting, different or funny? Try to grab the viewer in the first few seconds.

Engaging content tells a story and reveals something new. Think about the story or the 'narrative arc'. You may want to consider the beginning, middle, and end. Or perhaps you will be setting the scene, introducing something, and then paying it off.

When writing your video script, try to write it as a story, both in the script you are shooting to and the text box below the video. Treat that space like a blog post and tell the story you have shared in the video. The viewer may have had a short wait for the video to load. Give them a reason to hang around in the first few seconds. Make sure the title is snappy and your intro short. Say what you need to in the simplest possible way. Use supporting imagery to supplement your words but speak descriptively as if people are only listening.

Knowing and conversing with your audience

As with any piece of content to share, you need to know your audience to pitch the piece at the right level. Is your audience looking for a new piece of information, for entertainment or for escape? It is possible that a little of all three will be more engaging than focusing on facts and facts alone. Follow the mantra that if you can inspire, you will engage. A particularly effective way to engage with your audience is through a conversation. Remember, you are planning to share your content into a social space. If you ask a question you will most likely get a response, either in the comments below, or via other contact details you may share. Creating a conversation enhances the shared experience and gets people both talking and sharing your content. This will aid your video in reaching a much wider audience.

What makes a video viral?

Nobody knows the secret formula for making viral videos – that is, videos shared exponentially via social platforms in an infectious manner. It is a hard system to game. Yet, people are forever trying to engage with emotions in the hope they can reach communities far outside of their networks. A few commonalities in videos that have gone viral are as follows:

- Easy to share – sometimes the Twitter re-tweet or Facebook 'Like' button is enough. The key is to have one click sharing.
- Not a blatant advert – if it looks like an advert in the first few seconds, many will be put off.
- A parody of something popular – humour can be contagious and encourage sharing.
- Handheld – the 'run-and-gun' style of videoing adds drama and a live-action feel.
- Targeted to a particular audience – musicians have a lot of success sharing videos among their fans.
- A timed launch – well-thought-out timing can gain momentum fast.
- Easy to find – sometimes videos have been hosted on their own sites, within existing communities.
- Short – a short video is easier to download, digest, and share.

Sharing your finished videos

Social video apps and platforms come and go. Many start-ups begin with the best intentions but fall by the wayside, struggling to find the balance between community and commodity. When looking for somewhere to post your video content, it is a good idea to focus on the social video platforms that are part of something bigger or have proven business models.

YouTube

If you want your video content to be seen and heard, you should have a presence on platforms like YouTube. YouTube is the largest source of online videos in the world and claims to have over a billion users. On mobile alone it reaches more 18–49-year-olds than any cable network in the USA [source: https://www.youtube.com/yt/press/en-GB/statistics.html] and six out of ten people prefer online video platforms to TV [https://www.thinkwithgoogle.com/infographics/video-trends-where-audience-watching.html]. In addition, there are 1.2 trillion Google searches per year worldwide [http://www.internetlivestats.com/google-search-statistics/]. Within all of those searches is the option to view relevant videos.

YouTube has an app that makes easy work of capturing and uploading. Sometimes you may want to post a simple clip, such as an update, a fact or a video response to an online question. There are a number of simple-to-use mobile-based apps that can help you with this.

Bambuser

Launched in 2007, Bambuser is an interactive live-streaming video service. It works both on a mobile device and in the browser of a laptop or PC equipped with a webcam. While streaming video to various social platforms, viewers can comment in a chatroom alongside the video. This chat appears on the screen of the recording device. When bandwidth is tight, Bambuser has the ability to stream low-resolution video, replacing it with a higher-resolution version once a better connection is found. This function has made the service popular with mobile citizen reporters and activists around the world.

Periscope

Twitter acquired Periscope in 2015. Periscope users can record live video with the option to tweet out a link to their live stream. This video can be viewable to a selection of users or to all. Viewers can comment in real-time, adding 'hearts' that float up the screen to show appreciation. The video quality of Periscope is less than that of Bambuser, but its integration with Twitter means the user base and capacity to share are much larger. Using Periscope is a good way to reach those outside of your network.

Instagram

In 2012, Facebook bought Instagram for US$1 billion. Initially a photo sharing service, video recording was integrated into the service in June 2013. Users can record and share video from 3 to 60 seconds long as well as broadcast content to their network in real-time. Live streaming was added to the 'Stories' section of Instagram. Once you stop recording, the video is not archived but can be saved.

Twitter

As well as photos, the micro-blogging platform now allows up to 2 minutes and 20 seconds of video to be shared within a tweet.

Google Hangouts

Hangouts are an addition to the social layer G+ and Google's solution for video conferencing for up to ten people. Hangouts are both text chat and video call. 'Hangouts On-Air' enable you to create a live webcast within Google Plus where you can record and stream live into YouTube as well as Google Plus.

Facebook Live

As well as sharing video files into Facebook, the app enables you to stream live and interact in real-time with all or some of your Facebook network. You can ask questions or tell stories that will be archived on your page like any other Facebook post. A single broadcast can last up to 4 hours should you have the battery capacity. As with any live stream, a decent connection speed is also vital. 4G or a strong Wifi connection will enable you to deliver a continuous video stream. People can discover videos in their news feeds or subscribe to get notifications next time you go live.

Using and interpreting YouTube analytics

Research project funders and project evaluators will ask for statistics concerning your videos or audio content. If you have uploaded your content to YouTube, you can easily check the number of views in the view counter. In addition, there are a few other statistics that you can check.

I rarely click beyond the analytics 'Overview' page. This contains all the vital information and tells me if anyone is interested in my video experimentation.

Demographics

If you wish to dig a little deeper, another section of YouTube analytics is the demographics tab. This will allow you to customize your content according to the cross-section of viewers' ages.

Playback location, traffic sources, and devices

This is where you discover where and how your videos are viewed on the YouTube page, embedded in a site and through which devices. I'm used to views of my content through mobiles and PC but was surprised to see a few of my videos also being viewed on games consoles. This analytic will give you an insight into how people are finding you as well as where and how your videos are being shared.

Audience retention

This tab lets you know how interesting your content is. If your views are dropping off towards the end of the video, you either need to shorten the video or, better still, condense it and up the pace. You can also see which bits people are watching again.

The 'View Duration' is an average viewing percentage when compared with other similar-sized YouTube videos – the higher the percentage the better, with 65–70 per cent being pretty good. The first 10 seconds of any video are the most important. If you haven't hooked your viewer by then, they will be off exploring another part of the web.

Engagement report

You may have noticed an increase in YouTubers begging for subscriptions while pointing to a flashing action button on the screen. If done badly this can be annoying, but there is a reason for their eagerness. Subscribers = fans and they are the people most likely to share your videos to other places. More subscribers = an increased number of regular viewers coming back for more. A subscriber finds your videos in their email inbox, their YouTube feed, and via mobile notifications. Your Engagement Report will inform you of how many subscribers, comments, and likes your videos are getting, plus how the sharing is happening.

Between video and audio

There is also the 'halfway-house' approach to video. By adding photos to your audio and creating a photo-slideshow, you have a very professional media package that is easier to produce than video. Apps like VRP7 enable you to record some audio and then save a single image to that audio file – I call this an 'enhanced photo'. This can be saved to your phone's camera roll and shared as a short video. You can also add multiple images into an iMovie project on desktop or in the mobile app. You can then decide whether to add a voice-over or pre-recorded audio and save it as a video.

This technique works well if you want to explain presentation slides or a general viewpoint. It also works if someone would prefer not to appear on video. I like to capture an interview or soundbite and add that to a single image, or a series of photos. This can be assembled in an app and saved as a video to share in all the usual social places. Enhanced photos or photo slideshows are smaller in size than video and easier to upload and download [https://vimeo.com/22813997].

Tips and strategies for self-produced audio content

Knowing how to capture great audio will help you create better videos. But there may be times when audio is all you need. Having said that, video and audio work well together. You should always consider how both these media are able to fit into your content strategy.

The key benefits of sharing audio content

Audio files are smaller in size than video files. This enables stories rich in context to be shared in areas of low bandwidth and intermittent connectivity. In addition, audio clips can be easily shared as a podcast on Twitter or via a Really Simple Syndication (RSS) feed.

While videos demand the viewers' direct attention, audio is less demanding. The listener can digest podcasts in the car, on the move, or anywhere where multi tasking is needed. Also, unlike videos, audio content can be intimate. While it is easy to glance at a webpage and pick out the bits we like, it is harder to skim through audio. And when you are plugged into it, you feel immersed. I also believe that audio can deliver a story straight into your listeners' imagination. Audio sets the scene. It gives depth, personality, and emotion. This is then enhanced in the listeners' minds by their internal visuals as you take them on a journey. The American comic Steve Allen is reported to have said that 'Radio is the theatre of the mind; television is the theatre of the mindless.' This is because words and sounds can be more than enough to engage the imagination. When the listener adds visuals with their mind's eye, they create a personal visualization of the story.

From the production perspective, audio is easier to edit than video. The files are smaller and require less processing power. Audio can be edited on your phone with apps like VRP7 or Ferrite. It can also be edited on all desktop platforms with the free software called Audacity.

Sharing audio content

Podcasting and audio blogging

The word podcast originates from a mash-up of the words 'iPod' and 'broadcast'. In the 1980s, podcasting was known as audio blogging. A podcast is essentially a multimedia digital file made available on the internet for downloading to a PC or mobile device. Podcasts are some of the oldest episodic/syndicated content on the web. They make heavy use of RSS and the eXtendable Markup Language (XML) protocol. With RSS you can syndicate or subscribe to the feed of a website, blog and/or multimedia content hosted on the web. XML actually does very little, apart from structure, transport, and store information so that HTML can display it.

If your audio has an RSS feed, add yourself to the relevant podcasting directories – iTunes is by far the most popular. Some universities have their own platforms for multimedia podcasting. Purchase a unique URL that links to your podcast. For less than US$10 you can buy domain names from companies like NameCheap.com. It's then simple to forward that domain name to wherever your podcast resides. That way you are only sharing MemorablePodcastURL.com and not LongComplicatedName/User/Content/PodcastServiceName.com.

Until recently, the world of podcasting was dominated by audio. Increases in bandwidth and the evolution of portable devices have seen multimedia podcasting take over the scene. If people can subscribe and be sent your audio package, you are podcasting in the true sense of the word. If you are sharing audio into a social stream for people to listen to and share, you are closer to audio blogging.

Audio blogging and podcast tips

The following tips can help you gain momentum, hone skills, and build your audience with audio.

Content and style

Podcasting is about personality. When it comes to connecting, person-to-person, video can have the edge. You can be seen, and by looking into the lens you are engaging directly with the viewer. With audio, however, you'll need to get to know your listeners and let them get to know you. Social audio requires audience participation. Ask your community to feedback and comment. Including their input and feedback in future audio updates strengthens your community.

Even though you might be considering using just audio in your podcast, uploading cover art to your feed will help you get noticed. As mentioned before, apps like VRP7 enable you to share audio plus a photo in the shape of a video file. Once in this format, it can be uploaded to platforms like Twitter and Facebook. Your 'enhanced photo' will have the visual appearance of a video. People may want to find out more; a blog or webpage linking to further resources will enable you to deliver rich-data-filled information and stories. You can even include a 'call to action' in the description, and the comments section should also be close to hand.

Length

People will most likely find time to listen during a commute, or when they are doing something else. A 15–25 minute podcast can fit into someone's daily routine. If your podcast is longer than 45 minutes, then you are asking for a larger chunk of someone's day. Audio of seconds or minutes can be a simple way of adding your own view to a social update.

Regularity

Posting a regular podcast keeps momentum in your subscribing community. Interest is amplified, as you are kept fresh and relevant in the minds of your listeners. Aim for weekly rather than monthly podcasts; daily may be a little too frequent for long audio, but is fine for smaller audio chunks being shared into micro-blogging platforms.

Audience

Encourage your listeners to rate your podcast in iTunes. Ask them to share it via word of mouth and social channels. You could also offer your content and audio musings to other podcasts, blogs or radio shows. Also, don't forget to mention your podcast when interviewed on panels or in the media.

Sharing podcasts

Podcasts are not as sharable as an animated GIF or YouTube video. This is changing though. When impressed by an online video, all the tools and share buttons are there on the page. With podcasts, you might be listening on your phone, or in a podcatcher or an app. On the whole when sharing a link to a podcast, you are linking to its start. You might be asking someone to listen to 12 minutes of audio, setting the scene, before that inspirational nugget makes itself heard. It is for this reason (outside of music of course) that audio rarely goes viral. However, it does go viral – just not as often as visual formats.

Platforms like Audioboom and Soundcloud deliver embed codes and sharable links. These give users familiar-looking media players that easily plug into social platforms. Combined with a photo and the dynamic waveform, audio can be as attractive to click on as a video embed.

Here are a few tips for getting a clean sound for your audio projects:

- Choose quiet surroundings. For example, a place with soft furnishings absorbs sound and would work well.
- Get your subject close to the mic and turn off anything that may create background noise.
- During production, attaching a mic to your device can improve the quality of your audio and quieten background interruptions.

Editing your podcast

In post-production, some sound issues and artefacts can be corrected with desktop software such as Audacity. Capturing extra background audio at the time of the shoot can assist with the edit, as it's useful for smoothing transitions and isolating hums or drones from your final piece.

The importance of backing up

A few years ago I made, viewed, and shared social videos on Seesmic.com, 12seconds.tv and Phreadz.com. For one reason or another, the sites failed to be sustainable. Thousands of my videos got lost as servers were unplugged. I learnt an important lesson: it isn't just hard drive failures that you have to look out for. If you care about the photos, audio, video, and text you are creating, back it up.

Many start-ups do not have your best interests at heart – they are businesses looking to make money. Stuck with continually evolving business models, they are not sure if they'll be funded next year, let alone for the next 10 years. No matter how important your stories are to you, they are just data to them. I tend to think that my data is not safely archived unless it is in three different places. That way, if one fails, I can create another backup on the most up-to-date storage medium.

Video files take up a lot of drive space, but storage is getting cheaper and more stable. I use Networked Attached Storage (NAS), DVDs, individual hard drives, and 'The Cloud' (Dropbox). Take the time to protect your data and ensure your audio and video stories will be safe to inspire others now and into the future.

Newsletters

Newsletters can be a way of sharing your content on a regular basis with your subscribers. At the time of writing, one of the industry leaders in this area is

Mailchimp. I started my newsletter in 2016 with the simpler Mailchimp option called TinyLetter. I soon saw the benefits and upgraded to the fully featured Mailchimp. People see an interesting email as something packaged for them. Especially if you are delivering value and not just selling your wares. My newsletters have created a focused network who regularly offer help and advice. Several people from this network have even offered me places to stay as I work around the world. Then, of course, there is the work that comes from reminding people what it is that you do. Many of my workshop bookings come from replies to my newsletters.

Some tips for managing your newsletters

I have steadily grown my subscriber base. The service is free on Mailchimp up to 2,000 subscribers. With the in-depth analytics I can rate my readers on how engaged they are, sometimes chiselling away the casual browsers or those that don't open the email, thus keeping the service free. My newsletter is not viewable outside of email. Most are open to the public web with all articles linkable. I recommend you mention your newsletter in your social profiles and in email signatures to raise awareness.

Common Pitfalls

- Remember that live streaming is live and content is final. Only capture and share content from people with their consent. You will need to ask people for permission in areas where there is an expectation of privacy.
- If you have a tendency to ramble, it is a good idea to storyboard or script your audio or video productions. Keep pre-recorded content as short and concise as possible. Live streams will weave in and out audience participation. Finish them with the mention of a website or call to action.
- Fear of failure is a real block to getting creative online. It is important you give yourself a place to experiment with content creation. For example, it is possible to live stream to a single person on Facebook. Try creating a 'sandbox' where you can get a feel for things.

Best Practice

- Open access publishing of video and audio files makes your research and content sharable. This can build reputation and grow your network.
- High-quality content can be captured, created, and shared from your mobile device.
- A steady camera, shooting in good light, and capturing clear sound will be more appealing to your community.
- Capturing multimedia will drain more power than normal use. Make sure you have all the power you need. Carry a spare battery if necessary.

- When shooting video, natural, diffused light from an overcast day will get you better results over high contrast sunshine.
- As a rule keep the light behind you but don't cast a shadow on your subject.
- Try not to use zoom. Most mobile devices zoom digitally not optically. This eats into pixels, reducing image quality.
- Bad sound makes a bad video but good sound can also be a podcast.
- Engage. Live video thrives on interaction. Read the real-time comments and mention the viewers by name.
- Newsletters are still popular ways of rallying your community around your work. People appreciate a personal update direct to their inbox.

Cited resources

Bambuser [https://bambuser.com/]
Facebook Live [https://live.fb.com/]
Google Hangouts [https://hangouts.google.com/]
Instagram [https://www.instagram.com/]
Periscope [https://www.pscp.tv/]
Twitter [https://twitter.com/]
YouTube [https://www.youtube.com/]

Conclusion

Oliver Quinlan and Natalia Kucirkova

A digitally agile researcher can mean many things. As the authors in this volume have shown, there are many opportunities to be taken advantage of by using digital tools. It is not just a case of making use of some tools though, but rather taking part in a growing digital culture that research communities are becoming a part of. This necessitates some changes, thinking of your own digital identity as a brand as O'Byrne advises, moving from viewing interactions with your research as conversations with the public, or even creating new digital content such as audio, video apps as Kucirkova describes.

Digitally agile research takes some planning, it takes some thinking about what you want to gain, what opportunities you want to surface, and what challenges you are willing to rise to in your efforts to become a digitally agile researcher. This is why this book is themed around digital 'agility' and not just digital 'competence'. Take the time to do this work and develop the practical skills set out in the chapters and you will be able to engage in an agile way with the digital environments that are available to you, and to use them in an integrated way not just to share your research, but explore new approaches to it.

Through this book, the authors have provided practical ideas about how to develop your practice in engaging with digital culture, and making it beneficial for your own research. As the book concludes, we want to pull together some of the key ideas and thoughts to support you on your journey to digital public engagement.

The first and most important piece of advice is to set aside some time to sit down and plan what you want to get out of your approach to digital agility. No doubt the preceding chapters will have made you aware of new possibilities, and added more depth to those you already understood. However, to action the advice in all of them would be a daunting undertaking, and some will likely not be appropriate for your context. At this point, we would all do well to heed the advice of James Borrell, quoted by Ware and Parker in Chapter 5, that digital communications should not be undertaken 'at the expense of doing the science'. Taking a broad view of what you want to achieve and planning for it can ensure that your engagement with digital cultures is focused, meaningful, and adds to the core role of your research. However, as part of the plan, do set aside some time for experimentation, and be ready to consider serendipitous opportunities that several of our authors assert that engaging with digital culture can bring. In fact, a clear plan will help you to decide when to take advantage of these opportunities and when to pass them over, depending on how they fit with the goals you have defined. For example, an unexpected invitation to write about your research in a timely link to current news for a high-quality site such as

The Conversation is likely to fit with most of such plans, but an endless stream of guest blog posts for less well-read and regarded blog aggregators may be something you had better pass up in order to focus on actually doing your research.

Once you have made your plan, consider your digital identity as O'Byrne suggests in Chapter 2. Evaluate the online profile that likely already exists by searching for your own name online, and compare what you find with what you have planned to achieve. See this as something you will build up over time, and begin sharing content along these lines on a regular basis to slowly grow your profile in the way you are aiming for. Creating a single 'hub' that provides the definitive touchpoint for those who are looking to engage with you is highly recommended. View this as the starting point for building your 'cyber infrastructure'. If you set aside some time to slowly digitize your workflows, these new approaches can be built into your day-to-day work and not be a sudden set of new tools. O'Byrne's advice to see this development of practice as working smarter not harder is something we should all heed. Entering a new area will likely have an initial outlay of effort needed to fully explore, understand, and integrate them into your work. However, if you find they are taking vast amounts of time, you will need to evaluate whether they are reaching the goals you planned for. If they are not, then drop them, or at least evolve them into a more manageable role. If they are, then you need to consider what other things you should spend less time on or make more efficient so that they can happen. For example, you might start writing regular newsletters but you find over time that they are not that widely read or that people only read the first few lines. You may decide to drop the newsletters and spend your time on other engagement. It seems unlikely that the answer to the question of what to drop is ever your research or your writing, tempting that digital engagement can be sometimes as a procrastination tool.

Digital tools really do not have to be an extra, and Wheeler demonstrates in Chapter 3 how they can be integrated into a research process, not only approached at the end for research dissemination purposes. He urges readers to think specifically of social media as a data-gathering tool, something that can be a part of your research at several stages. To realize this you may need to start to build a network of your own, and joining Twitter chats related to your work can be a productive way to start to discover large numbers of people that it would be beneficial to correspond with. You should also consider how this network could help you tap into the literature on new subjects, whether by sharing questions that others may have read around already, or by finding sources of literature that can inform your reviews. It is important to consider copyright when using sources from online publications, so be sure to know what the key issues involved in this are before using the sources. You can also use social media as a more primacy source, reaching out to research subjects through surveys, or directly for interviews. Do be sure to consider the differences in online and offline behaviour when doing this, and keep both ethics and issues of reliability and validity at the centre of your thinking.

Much social media is short form, making it ideal for forging conversations and building networks. Conversations can build around a topic, and differing views can result in useful discussions. However, much academic work involves a complexity of ideas, especially while a project is in progress. For setting out and exploring more complex ideas, blogs are a key online tool. They are often depicted as a way to do traditional *post hoc* research engagement. However, in Chapter 4, Gombrich shows how a blog can be an active tool to develop ideas and explore one's understanding of topics. Much traditional communication that researchers get involved in is polished, but he advises researchers to take a more experimental writing style or even playful approach to their blogs. Many people hesitate starting a blog, as they are unsure what the voice they wish to convey is, and how they will structure their work in this new context. It's like the blank page syndrome we face when starting to write in any new context. Although a blog should definitely form part of the plan you make following O'Byrne's advice, overly structuring your view of what a blog should be can diminish its potential as a space for developing ideas and garnering feedback. See it as a first draft, one that will be refined with experience and feedback, a conversation starter rather than a definitive presentation of your findings. Although a blog could form a place to let people know about more final works, Gombrich's experience shows how it can be used to develop new ideas that could later feed into that work, and to build a network of discussion around these early ideas. A key point from his chapter to remember in the current world of social media celebrity is that it isn't all about the numbers. The quality of connections you can make from a blog, or any online media for that matter, is more important than amassing vast numbers of views or reactions, and even small numbers engaging with your work can lead to surprising opportunities to take the ideas in new directions, or even to work with others on the next stage of those ideas or your career.

Having invested a lot of time in developing as an academic, writing in an engaging, persuasive, and simple manner can be a change, and Ware and Parker have many tips on developing this side to your writing in Chapter 5. Appropriately as representatives of The Conversation, they also encourage you to see the online side of your work as starting a conversation around your ideas, findings, and process. Engaging online writing can benefit from certain styles that are more journalistic than the usual academic paper, particularly in terms of its immediacy. Rather than building an argument slowly, they advise getting readers' attention by presenting the key findings or questions you think are important, and then building their understanding of them through delving into the details. Traditional academic work requires a certain detachment and time-distance, but in the online world timeliness can be a key concept, so thinking about how your work fits with the current discourses that are taking place among your communities and audiences is crucial. Ware and Parker extend Gombrich's and Wheeler's advice by focusing on some key and very practical tips for disseminating academic research rather than the more developmental writing and engagement previously described. The sequence of the chapters is deliberate so that ideas are made to flow from one to the next. Having said that, for some researchers it may make sense to start the next stage of their digital journey by taking The Conversation dissemination route, before exploring more developmental territory.

With blogs, their uses can range from developing ideas to their dissemination. With social media, the research benefits can range from building a critical network of co-researchers to gathering new research data. Many tools can be used for many ends depending on what is needed. As Kucirkova explores in Chapter 6, smartphones are no different, and are in fact some of the most flexible tools to consider in your plan for digital agility. The personal technology revolution of the last 10 years has made these powerful and portable tools highly available and mobile devices can be rich sources for collecting research data. Before you adopt them for your research, think about the ethical and practical issues concerning the ownership of both the devices and the data collected on them. With these issues addressed, you can capture data on their use or audio and video of interviews or observations. Depending on the subject of your research, you could consider creating an app that tests certain interactions or behaviours, and Kucirkova gives a detailed example of how she worked with colleagues to do this to explore the subject of young children's reading and story-making. If you are not familiar with the potential of mobile apps, it is well worth considering and exploring how they may aid you in your research process. Building an app is a larger and more costly undertaking than most of the other practices described in this book, but it is getting more and more accessible and for the right projects can be a hugely useful part of the research process.

A research element that has been fundamentally transformed by digital technology is access to information. In Chapter 7, Dowson shares advice on how to effectively manage and take advantage of the vast array of tools to access information and research literature. Sometimes the skillset of searching and finding information can be neglected – in an age where everyone can use the Google search feature, it is easy to wrongly assume that search skills do not need development. Yet, a search strategy is one of the most important skills to underpin your research and Dowson has several tips for developing this. Regardless of how familiar you are with digital culture, this chapter is key to any digital agility, as it takes an area you will certainly be working on already and provides ideas for using tools that can save you time and help make your access to information even more comprehensive – and effective.

Developing your skills in a specific area such as finding information can, with some guidance, be a straightforward process. Developing your online presence and use of networking tools can be much more daunting owing to a lack of structure and the need to develop your own path through unfamiliar territory. Quinlan offers useful advice on creating a path through this territory, which is inherently different for different researchers depending on your focus and your field. He echoes earlier advice to both plan for your aims and to evaluate the presence you already have. Networking can seem like an alien pursuit to many of us involved in research, but you could re-frame it as a way of meeting potential collaborators with similar interests and/or different perspectives to bring to your work. The platforms you use for networking are so abundant now that it would be easy for a researcher to spend all their time on networking, so it is well worth evaluating which ones are likely to give you value. Depending on the stage of your career, these are likely to be different, and Quinlan offers some guidance on considering this question. The key thing is seeing online networking to stand for creating and gaining from engagement about your work. Whether you are sharing your finished research outputs, or the process and development of outputs, or looking to gather data, it is all about going beyond sharing, spotting engagement with what you have shared and encouraging further engagement and dialogue.

While many view engagement and conversations with the public as a part of the dissemination phase of their research, it is the engagement between research participants, recipients of research, and the researchers themselves that is the focus of Holliman and colleagues in Chapter 9. These authors share the practical experience of engaging with a range of stakeholders during the research process and taking a 'co-design' approach to research. The potential for digital technology to open up communication has some fascinating consequences for how research may develop well beyond the model of a 'passive observer', towards new roles, nurturing new understandings of research participants. Acting as digitally agile researchers, this team of authors shows the potential of how a well-developed understanding of digital culture can allow an exploration of new contexts in which research can take place, with new findings as a result. Ever digitally reflective, their work surfaces various models that can be used to structure future explorations of this kind of engagement.

In addition to using digital tools to propagate content, digital agility is also about creating your own digital content. In Chapter 10, Payne offers a wide range of tips for making the most of multimedia and ensuring that your outputs live up to the plans you have made for digital engagement. While previous chapters focused more on the written word, Payne foregrounds video and audio content production. All content production is bound by audience awareness and Payne outlines some tricks and strategies for creating relevant and engaging video and audio content. An average smartphone provides more than the needs of an average digital researcher, so audio/video production is not about the tools but rather how you use those tools to create content that is engaging and has the production values needed to develop the engagement you seek. Both video and audio can fulfil the need for content to spur conversation, and Payne guides you through the key steps of audio-visual story-telling, how to capture it with optimum clarity, and how to ensure that you are getting the most out of the technological devices at your disposal. Digital content doesn't have to be polished and final, indeed the misconception that it does is often the main thing stopping researchers from taking advantage of the potential they are more than capable of realizing.

Many authors have discussed how to develop your approach to digital agility, how to plan, and how to create aims for engaging with new media. Becoming truly digitally agile is undoubtedly about finding your own way through the opportunities and challenges that digital culture presents. Taking time to develop specific skills can give you the confidence and capability to create content that can take your research somewhere it would not have gone otherwise. This is the key theme of the book – using the digital as an integrated part of your work to take it places it would not have gone otherwise.

Superficial treatments of digital public engagement can be misconceptualized as to merely serve the purpose of proving some research impact. Yes, you can place summaries of your published papers on a blog and you might get some pleasing numbers to add to your impact reports and performance reviews. However, there is so much more that could be achieved with the potential of digital tools for communication, for finding and collaborating with peers, developing new workflows, and reaching out to research subjects and audiences. As the authors in this book demonstrate, digital public engagement is not about yet another thing to master and performatively engage with. Rather, digital public engagement is about the way of thinking and doing things, about the 'culture' that you can become a part of and that can influence the way you think about what you do.

The opportunities to become part of such a culture can seem too many and may appear too daunting. With a focused plan recommended by the authors here, it is possible to build digital engagement in a gradual and sustained way to the point that you are interacting in new ways and even discovering new directions to your research and to your career as a result. We hope this book will help you on this journey, in whatever small or big way you choose it to.

Index

How to Get a PhD
A Handbook for Students and their Supervisors
6th Edition

Estelle M. Phillips and Derek S. Pugh

ISBN: 978-0-335-26412-4 (Paperback)
eBook: 978-0-335-26413-1
2015

How to Get a PhD is the market leading, classic book for PhD students and their supervisors. It provides a practical, down to earth and realistic approach to studying for a PhD and offers support and reassurance for both students and supervisors. This new edition has been extensively updated to reflect changes in the HE sector, the PhD process and student demographics and behaviour.

Key features:

- Explores the nature of the PhD qualification
- Teaches how to manage your supervisors
- Examines challenges you may encounter throughout your PhD

www.openup.co.uk